# AVIATION
# INSECURITY

"At last! A sobering and comprehensive exposé about our nation's continuing vulnerabilities in airport security. Despite current government assurances of an effective and safe security framework, Thomas details security flaws and failures before 9/11 that inexplicably still prevail today. In this frightening examination, Thomas illuminates solutions and focuses on shortfalls that must be remedied if we are to thwart the potent threat of terrorism on the tarmac. This book sounds the alarm that America's airline passengers remain the unwitting and inadequately defended targets in the war against terror. A sobering must-read for anyone who travels by air."
—Deborah Sherman, Investigative Reporter, WTVJ-TV, Miami, Florida

"Thomas easily shows how quickly terrorists could turn to their own advantage the locked cockpit door. He demonstrates how to apply a systems approach, something we expected security designers to have done."
—Prof. Gerald P. Chubb
Department of Aerospace Engineering and Aviation, The Ohio State University

"A must-read for anyone who flies or pays taxes."
—Bob Monetti, President, The Victims of Pan Am Flight 103, Inc.

"Serves as a wake-up call to us all, continental United States and beyond, to ensure whatever measures we do take make security sense and respond appropriately to the threat posed. … [T]he governmental fanfare surrounding many of the new policies and technologies since put in place is a mere smoke screen and has done little to improve the situation."
—Philip Baum, Editor, *Aviation Security International*

"An important first step in the critical analysis of the events that allowed 9/11 to happen. The author outlines how Washington's overriding interest in the financial success of the airline industry and the industry's greed contributed to the lack of aviation security. It's a warning call to America to see through a tireless, dogged campaign to get it done right once and for all."
—Eric Grasser, Editor, *Airport Security Report*

"Explains how industry giants have masterfully manipulated Washington politicians, the FAA, and now the TSA into promoting the marketplace, rather than regulating the industry. While exploitable vulnerabilities in air travel are permitted to exist, we will continue to experience an 'aviation insecurity' problem of mass proportions. . . . Thomas's methods of astute analysis and rational problem solving are thought provoking."
—Mary Kahl, Board Member, National Air Disaster Alliance & Foundation

"Andrew Thomas is helping to lift the veil of secrecy protecting the airline industry and the government from the truth: The 9/11 hijackers exploited commonly known problems of lax security that were known and admitted to by the U.S. government and the airlines.

"Thomas explains how and why the U.S. government let the airlines hide the truck rather than cut back on corporate perks and profits and fix the problem."
—Mary Schiavo, Aviation Disaster Attorney
Former Inspector General, U.S. Department of Transportation

ANDREW R. THOMAS

# AVIATION
# INSECURITY

The New Challenges of Air Travel

Prometheus Books

59 John Glenn Drive
Amherst, New York 14228-2197

Published 2003 by Prometheus Books

Inquiries should be addressed to
Prometheus Books
59 John Glenn Drive
Amherst, New York 14228–2197
VOICE: 716–691–0133, ext. 207
FAX: 716–564–2711
WWW.PROMETHEUSBOOKS.COM

07 06 05 04 03    5 4 3 2 1

Library of Congress Cataloging-in-Publication Data

Reichert, Tom.
    Aviation insecurity : the new challenges of air travel / by Tom Reichert.
        p. cm.
    Includes bibliographical references and index.
    ISBN 1–59102–074–3 (pbk. : alk. paper)
    1. Aeronautics—Security measures—United States. 2. Air travel—United States. 3. September 11 Terrorist Attacks, 2001. I. Title.

TL552.52.R45 2003
363.28'76—dc21

                                                            2003001479

Printed in the United States of America on acid-free paper

*For my grandmother Thelma Thomas,*
*who taught me about the sacrifices necessary*
*to keep a people free.*

# CONTENTS

# CONTENTS

## PART 2. A NEW SET OF EYES

# ACKNOWLEDGMENTS

**A**ny book is the outcome of the efforts of several individuals whose selfless dedication is ultimately reflected in the finished product. In this case, a number of patriots from what I call the "aviation security accountability community" stepped up and answered the call without hesitation or the promise of reward or glory. The work done by Larry Costanzo of the Airline Investigation Unit was invaluable in setting up the first part of the book. The input, counsel, and confidence of Brian Sullivan, Steve Elson, and Bogdan Dzakovic will never be forgotten.

My agent, Wendy Keller, has been a source of inspiration for me, as I have seemingly struggled for many years to become an author. The time taken by my friends Ted Lux and Moe Aleman to review the manuscript was something of great personal value. My editors at Prometheus—Linda Regan, Chris Kramer, and Meg French—were instrumental in keeping me in line and on schedule.

The eighteen months I spent working on this book were a burden on my family. My wife, Jackie, always understood as the deadlines came and went and came again. The incredible interest expressed by my son , Paul Bryan, about this subject lifted me up when my spirits would get down. Alana, who was with me every day as I wrote this book, will hopefully appreciate one day why her dad spent so much time clicking and clacking on the keyboard while she graciously played in front of his desk. It is my children and the country they will inherit from me that compelled the writing of this book.

# PART I
# SET UP TO FAIL

# CHAPTER 1

# HOW COULD THIS HAVE HAPPENED?

" 'Our country, right or wrong...' Have you not perceived that that phrase is an insult to the nation? Only when a republic's life is in danger should a man uphold his government when it is in the wrong. There is no other time. This republic's life is not in peril."

—Mark Twain, from "Glances at History"

September 11 really wasn't that hard to pull off. Don't let anybody tell you otherwise. Contrary to what many will say, the idea didn't take a genius to dream up. The methods and tactics were not sophisticated. In fact, hijacking four commercial airliners and flying them into predetermined targets on the ground was pretty much a piece of cake.

Although the idea of getting into the cockpit of a commercial airliner seemed almost impossible to many, the opposite was actually quite true. Thirty passengers on flights around the world had already broken through cockpit doors during the twenty-four months leading up to 9/11. The plot to turn a plane into a flying bomb may have been difficult to imagine for most. Yet, it had already been threatened and put into action on several occasions. Others assumed that learning to fly a Boeing 757 or 767 into a target required years of study and practice. In reality, it was a skill that could have been picked up in about a week.

For years, the warning signs were everywhere. And, for years, the individuals and organizations we trusted *and* paid to protect us turned their heads. "Reinforce cockpit doors," it was suggested. "Can't. Too expensive," was the response. "Train better flight attendants to handle in-flight incidents," it was urged. "Can't. Too time-consuming and too expensive," was the response. "Prosecute disruptive passengers," was the plea. "Can't. Causes too many delays and time is money." "Create a seamless security system that ensures ease of movement and delivers high levels of protection for passengers," was the call. "Won't do that. There's no reason to."

Then, after the seemingly impossible occurred, we were told: "There was no way we could have predicted what happened." "We never thought hijackers would be suicidal." "How could we ever have known what they were going to do?" etc., etc.

For all of the excuses, denials, and doublespeak, the writing on the wall was extremely clear. Now, this may appear to be a lot of Monday-morning quarterbacking on the author's part, but the amount of evidence pointing to the strategic nature of the attacks and how easily the terrorists would execute them was there well before the four airliners took off from Boston, Newark, and Washington, D.C. The evidence is overwhelming and compels us to take another look.

## EVIDENCE THAT DEMANDS A VERDICT

When trying to understand 9/11 for what it really was—a low-tech, but extremely effective strike on the United States—the known targets and the methods used allow us to see what the terrorists were trying to accomplish. Further, by analyzing what happened, we can see inward as to the failings of our intelligence and aviation security systems that led to that fateful day.

The World Trade Center (WTC) and the Pentagon were obviously critical to the American way of life on 9/11. The WTC was not just a symbol of U.S. economic power around the globe, it was also home to some of the most important financial services firms in the world. The Pentagon, beyond its metaphorical significance as the icon of U.S. military power, is also the nerve center of the armed forces. And, to restate the obvious, the aviation system in the United States is critical to our economic well-being as a nation. Civil aviation in general and commercial aviation in particular account for somewhere around 9 percent of the total gross domestic product of the United States. That is more than $900 billion. In addition, upwards of 11 million jobs are related directly, indirectly, and, through induced spending and hiring, to commercial aviation.[1]

To recognize and truly grasp what happened on that day, two sets of facts must be examined first: the large volume of intelligence warnings our government received in the months leading up to 9/11 and the indisputable proof that suicidal hijackers taking over a commercial aircraft and slamming it into a predetermined target was already a viable option.

## The Intelligence Breakdown

The body of information on the intelligence failings of 9/11 is growing exponentially and will most certainly be a topic of hot debate for years to come. Of the two sets of facts, the one focusing on the intelligence warnings has been the most widely reported and discussed since the attacks. It is not my intention to completely restate what several analysts before me have already done so well.[2] Although intelligence and aviation security are intricately linked, the primary focus of this book is on the aviation security system, not the U.S. intelligence community. In many ways, however, the aviation security system is a client of the intelligence apparatus. Aviation threats discovered by the intelligence community are supposed to be passed along to those who set security policy so that any necessary adjustments to the system can be made. However, prior to 9/11, it was apparent that the client wasn't always being served very well.

### What Did They Know and When Did They Know It?

House and Senate hearings trying to answer the question, "What did Bush administration officials know and when did they know it?" made headlines throughout 2002. Many observers compared the inquiries to similar ones that were held after the Japanese attack at Pearl Harbor on December 7, 1941. Then, as now, we wanted to get to the bottom of how this could happen and why.

Throughout both investigations, it was often said that the evidence for the attack was there but government leaders failed to connect the dots. President Roosevelt and other leaders of the government knew in mid-1941 that the Japanese military was up to something. Across Asia, Japan had tightened its stranglehold on China, Thailand, and other areas of Indochina. Japan was on the march and looking for more territory to gobble up. The great issues of the day were much less a question of "if" the Japanese were going to strike, but much more "where" and "when."

Serious historians and World War II buffs continue to argue whether President Roosevelt and his staff really knew of the Japanese fleet's order of battle in the winter of 1941. We now know that many in the government incorrectly concluded that the Japanese navy would attack the Dutch East Indies. Others thought possibly the Philippines. A few correctly predicted that the Japanese would strike at Pearl Harbor. The evidence remains unclear about what Roosevelt ultimately discerned from all of the divergent reports and analyses he received. What is certain, however, is that the government failed to create policies that would have guarded against an attack at Pearl Harbor and saved thousands of American lives.

Debate about the Bush administration's previous knowledge of the 9/11 attacks follows a similar pattern. In the weeks before September 11, federal officials were made aware of attack threats to the United States made by members of Al Qaeda, possibly using commercial aviation as the modus operandi. In early June 2001, when the leaders of the 'Group of 8' nations met for their annual meeting in Genoa, Italy, the government of Egypt sent a warning to the Bush administration about a possible suicide hijacker. In an interview with the French newspaper *Le Figaro*, Egyptian President Hosni Mubarak said he had uncovered a video where Osama bin Laden "spoke of assassinating President Bush and other heads of state in Genoa . . . using an airplane stuffed with explosives." To respond to this potential threat, anti-aircraft missile batteries were placed around the city during the summit.[3]

On June 28, 2001, National Security Advisor Condoleezza Rice received an intelligence summary warning that a significant Al Qaeda attack in the near future was "highly likely." One week later, on July 5, National Security Council terrorism chief Richard Clarke convened a White House meeting of the Counterterrorism Security Group (CSG). Later that same day, Clarke met with Rice and Bush's Chief of Staff Andrew Card. Following that meeting, another CSG session was held, which this time included representatives from the Federal Aviation Administration (FAA), Federal Bureau of Investigation (FBI), and Immigration and Naturalization Service (INS). Clarke told them, "Something spectacular is going to happen."

What begins to emerge is eerily similar to what was going on in Washington during the days prior to Pearl Harbor. The question "if" had nearly been answered. "When" and "where" were what remained.

On July 18, the FAA warned the airlines to exercise the highest level of caution. Thirteen days later, on July 31, the FAA advised the airlines that terrorists were planning and training for hijackings.[4] On August 17, the INS detained Zacarias Moussaoui for suspicious activity at a Minnesota flight school. He was later identified as the twentieth hijacker for the 9/11 attacks. On September 4, a week before the attacks, the FBI told the FAA of Moussaoui's arrest. However, the FAA did not alert the airlines.

The government's explanations in the days and months following the attacks were predictable. On September 17, 2001, recently appointed FBI Director S. Robert Mueller III insisted his agency "had no warning signs" of the previous week's attacks. When asked by a reporter at a news conference whether the federal government had ever anticipated a 9/11-type attack, Ari Fleischer, White House press secretary, said, "I don't think this should come as any surprise to anybody," speaking of the warnings given to President Bush months before the attacks. "But the president did not—not receive information about the use of airplanes as missiles by suicide bombers. This was a new type of attack that was not foreseen."[5]

In a press conference the next day at the White House, Rice concurred. "The government did everything that it could—in a period in which the information was very generalized, in which there was nothing specific in which to react— and had this president known of something more specific or known that a plane was going to be used as a missile, he would have acted on it."[6] The administration Fleischer and Rice were working for was either incredibly inexperienced or spinning its own version of the truth. The fact is, enough of the dots were already connected so that a definable picture was beginning to come forth.

Still, to be fair, knowing exactly when and where terrorists will strike was and remains quite difficult to determine. The ease of movement the terrorists enjoyed both inside and outside of the U.S. prior to 9/11 made it challenging for even the best analyst to accurately predict their plans and intentions. So, apparently, was keeping track of two of the hijackers who eventually boarded American Airlines Flight 77 and crashed it into the Pentagon. According to published reports, the CIA knew that Nawaf Alhazmi and Khalid Al-Midhar were in the United States and that they were connected to Al Qaeda. For nearly twenty-one months after they were identified by the CIA as terrorists, Alhazmi and Al-Midhar lived openly in the United States, using their real names, getting driver's licenses, opening bank accounts, and attending flight schools.[7]

Incredibly, the CIA did nothing with the information. They notified neither the FBI, which could have tracked down the two men, nor the INS, which could have turned them away at the Canada-U.S. border. Al-Midhar, remarkably, was able to obtain a multiple-entry visa from the U.S. Embassy in Saudi Arabia that allowed him to enter and leave the United States at will. When Al-Midhar's visa expired, the State Department issued him a new one in July 2001, even though the CIA had linked him to one of the suspected bombers of the *USS Cole* in Yemen in October 2000.[8]

To blame only the Bush administration for the intelligence failures would be disingenuous, however. The Clinton administration also missed much of what was so obvious as well. With the exception of Rice, it is a sad fact that President Bush's intelligence team was composed almost entirely of Clinton administration holdovers or career bureaucrats promoted by these same holdovers. There was no transition or changes in personnel at the CIA when the new administration took office in 2001. Likewise at the FBI, Louis Freeh and his handpicked deputies were kept on with no changes after Bush's inauguration in January.[9]

So the simple truth remains. The American people were let down by their leaders in many ways throughout the 1990s and into the new century when it came to interpreting what many saw as an inevitability. This is clear. And it can be seen by looking at how many of the dots had already been connected before 9/11.

## Warnings from Other Governments

Beyond the warning from Egypt that was received prior to the "G8 Summit," several other governments had notified Washington of increased Al Qaeda activity and the rising specter of an attack on the United States. According to press reports in Russia, Russian intelligence notified the CIA during the summer of 2001 that twenty-five terrorist pilots had been specifically geared toward suicide missions. In an interview on September 15 with MSNBC, Russian President Vladimir Putin confirmed that he had ordered Russian intelligence in August to warn the U.S. government "in the strongest terms" of imminent attacks on airports and government buildings. Earlier in June, the BND, the German intelligence service, warned the CIA and Israel that Middle Eastern terrorists were "planning to hijack commercial aircraft to use as weapons to attack important symbols of American and Israeli culture."[10]

After putting all of this together, it would not be too much of a stretch to indict both the Bush and Clinton administrations for failing to perform their due diligence when it came to handling the intelligence prior to 9/11. The players were known, the targets well defined, the method delineated. Yet, time after time, when something could have been done, little or no action was taken by our government's leaders to thwart this rising and very real threat.

## An Aircraft as a Flying Missile

The notion of a suicidal hijacker turning an aircraft into a flying missile is not a novel idea. Those who claimed they couldn't have imagined such a scenario need only to look at how such an act had been threatened or accomplished in the past. Before the 1996 Summer Olympics in Atlanta, intelligence officials at the FBI and CIA had identified crop dusters and suicide flights as potential terrorist threats and took steps to prevent any attack from the air during the games. Black Hawk helicopters and Customs Service jets were deployed to intercept suspicious aircraft in the skies over Atlanta. Law enforcement agents monitored crop dusters and fanned out across the region "to make sure nobody hijacked a small aircraft and tried to attack one of the venues," said Woody Johnson, the FBI agent in charge of the Atlanta office at the time.[11]

In 1995, the FBI was warned of a terrorist plot to hijack several commercial airliners and slam them into the Pentagon and the CIA headquarters in Langley, Virginia. In January of that year, a fire in the Manila apartment building of Abdul Murad and Ramzi Yousef led Philippine investigators to uncover a plot to plant timed explosive devices on several U.S. airliners. The bomb-making equipment police found in the apartment led to Murad, who was then captured in Manila. Yousef was out of the country at the time. During intense and often brutal interrogations by Philippine authorities, Murad told of detailed plans to simultaneously blow up several planes over the Pacific Ocean while he and another suicide hijacker would each carry out a kamikaze suicide attack on the CIA and Pentagon respectively.[12]

Later that same year, Yousef, the ringleader of the of the first World Trade Center bombing in 1993, was arrested in Pakistan and turned over to the United States. On his flight back to the U.S. for trial, Yousef reportedly told FBI agent Brian Parr and other agents guarding him that he had narrowly missed several opportunities to blow up a dozen airliners over the Pacific in one single day and carry out a suicide attack on CIA headquarters.[13] It is still unclear whether this compelling information was ever disseminated to other security agencies.

In December 1994 an Air France flight in Algiers, Algeria, was hijacked by the Armed Islamic Group. The hijackers ordered the plane flown to Marseilles, in the south of France, where it landed. They ordered authorities to load an additional twenty-seven tons of aviation fuel for a journey to Paris, although the trip required only about one-third that amount. The hijackers' aim was to crash the plane into the Eiffel Tower. While still on the ground in Marseilles, commandos from French special forces stormed the plane.

Exactly seven years before the attacks, during the late night hours of September 11, 1994, a distraught, unemployed student pilot named Frank Eugene Corder stole a Cessna from Aidino Airport in Churchville, Maryland. Corder, who was reportedly an alcoholic and crack addict, flew to Washington, entering the prohibited airspace around the White House just before 2 A.M. After passing low over the Ellipse, he dove toward the White House and crashed on the lawn just south of the executive mansion.

In April 1994, Auburn Calloway, a flight engineer who was facing dismissal from his job at Federal Express, boarded one of the company's DC-10 cargo planes in Memphis. Traveling under the guise of an employee/passenger, Calloway waited until after the plane took off to storm the cockpit. Using a hammer, Calloway attacked the three pilots, bludgeoning each of them almost to death.

After taking over the plane, Calloway had planned to turn it into a flying missile and slam the aircraft into Federal Express's handling facility in Memphis. Fortunately, the three pilots eventually regained control of the aircraft from Calloway.[14]

## Suicide Pilots

As early as 1996, the FBI began investigating the activities of suspected Middle Eastern terrorists at U.S. flight schools. During that year, FBI agents visited several schools, including two attended by our bomb-making friend from the Philippines, Abdul Murad. In 1998, FBI agents questioned officials from Airman Flight School in Norman, Oklahoma, about a graduate identified in court testimony as a pilot for Osama bin Laden. This was the school later attended by Zacarias Moussaoui.[15]

With regard to the required skill level of the 9/11 terrorists who actually piloted the planes, Dr. Todd Curtis, one of the nation's foremost aviation safety experts and a pilot himself, explains that a little bit of training could go a long way. A few years ago, Dr. Curtis had the opportunity to take a short course on the 757 that included classroom training, individual computer-based training, and about five hours in a full-motion simulator.

According to Dr. Curtis, after about a week of training, he was familiar with the layout of the flight deck and with the operation of the flight controls, autopilot, and navigation systems. Flying the simulator was much less difficult than he had imagined at the beginning of the course.

The most difficult parts of the simulator training were takeoffs and landings. On the other hand, flying the aircraft in other phases of flight was relatively easy, even compared to flying a Cessna 172. Changing the aircraft's course, speed, or altitude was not very difficult when using either the autopilot system or when flying the aircraft manually. The flight control system made the aircraft rather responsive and made it easy to perform normal flying maneuvers.

Given his experiences in the simulator, Dr. Curtis felt that if he were to be put into a 757's cockpit in the middle of a flight on a relatively clear and sunny day, he would be able to change direction and altitude without any trouble. Given a basic knowledge of a region's geography and available navigational aids, he would also be able to navigate well enough that he could find a major city and fly the aircraft to any major landmark in that city. Because the basic cockpit layout and many of the procedures used in the 757 are almost identical to those of the 767, Dr. Curtis feels that the same would be true for a 767.[16] The ease of flying the aircraft may also have been aided on 9/11 by the use of global positioning systems (GPS) that the terrorists reportedly purchased a few weeks before the attacks.

## LEVERAGING COMMERCIAL AVIATION

The intelligence failure was not the only rupture that opened the door for the 9/11 attacks to take place. A well-conceived terrorist plan can succeed only when a system exists in such a vulnerable condition that terrorists can leverage several weaknesses to achieve their strategic objectives. Just because Al Qaeda types were making threats and overtures about hijacking planes and slamming them into buildings didn't mean it was going to happen. Real weaknesses in aviation security had to exist that could be exploited. If those deficiencies hadn't existed, commercial aviation would not have been used.

Commercial aviation served only as the delivery system for the havoc and destruction they sought to wreak. Had they been able to use a better, more effective, tactical method for achieving their strategic goals, I'm certain the 9/11 terrorists would have chosen it over commercial aviation. Yet, we knew for years that they had envisioned a suicidal hijacking of a commercial airliner, that it might very well maximize the impact of their actions. The results of 9/11 bear this out.

The human, economic, and psychological damage resulting from the suicide hijackings was not an end in itself. Instead, the death and destruction the attacks wrought were simply a means to a greater end. In bin Laden's *fatwa* of February 23, 1998, he urged Muslims around the world to join him in the fight against the enemies of God. Most certainly, bin Laden's ultimate objective for the 9/11 attacks was to elicit a massive response by the non-Muslim world on his brethren. U.S. involvement in Afghanistan, the Philippines, and now Iraq is exactly what bin Laden wanted. Moderate Arabs are finally beginning to question their governments' relationships with non-Muslim nations like the U.S. Further, events in Kashmir reveal Al Qaeda's desire to push India into an attack on Muslim Pakistan. Failing to recognize the global objectives of Al Qaeda, that is, to lure the non-Muslim world into war with the followers of Islam, is to negate why 9/11 really happened.

## The Psychological Damage from the 9/11 Attacks

The psychological damage of witnessing those planes slamming into the World Trade Center towers was incredible, almost incomprehensible. The 9/11 planners probably counted on at least one, some, or maybe that even all of the attacks would be captured on film. In addition, the planners most certainly knew the fires and destruction resulting from the attacks would be beamed around the world on live television. Seeing the Pentagon and twin towers on fire, followed by the towers' subsequent collapse right in front of our eyes was something nobody will ever forget. Even Osama bin Laden seemed surprised at the destruction when he intimated in a videotaped interview that his planners didn't expect the towers to fall. For nearly everybody, these were the first plane crashes we had ever witnessed. And we saw them over and over and over and over . . . like the replay of a great moment in sports or a famous scene from a movie.

At the time of this writing, studies currently under way in the New York area are beginning to show large percentages of children and adults suffering from some form of Post-Traumatic Stress Disorder (PTSD). In addition, studies suggest many of the recovery workers at the Pentagon and the World Trade Center are dealing with PTSD as well. Although much research needs to be undertaken, we can surely argue that the attacks met the terrorists' aim of achieving a high degree of psychological impact.

## The Human Impact

On a purely human scale, the tragedy of 9/11 was of historical dimension. Throughout United States history no single event has claimed more civilian lives than the 3,040 lost on September 11, 2001. The attack on Pearl Harbor, December 7, 1941, took 2,403 civilian and military lives. By comparison, the bloodiest day in U.S. history took place during the Civil War at the Battle of Antietam on September 17, 1862, where 4,032 soldiers died. Despite the tragedy of so many lives lost, analyses conducted after the 9/11 attacks concluded that many more lives could have been lost.

It appears that the evacuation of the World Trade Center was a success, as nearly everyone who could get out did get out.[17] Much of this success was due to the heroic efforts of the thousands of New York City rescue workers who ran toward the burning buildings, rather than away from them. The 479 rescue workers who perished—including firefighters, police officers, and Port Authority employees—made the ultimate sacrifice and undoubtedly helped others to survive.

According to several security professionals familiar with the WTC, evacuation procedures in place at both towers also helped save lives. After the 1993 WTC bombing, a combination of careful planning, education of building occupants, practice, and preparedness reduced the 9/11 death toll significantly. Specifically, a fire warden program was implemented that educated occupants of each floor about evacuation procedures. And evacuation chairs placed throughout the buildings for disabled people assisted them in getting out effectively. The time of the attacks also helped to reduce the casualties—the actual number of people in each tower was between five thousand and seven thousand, about half the total occupancy when the first jet struck at 8:46 A.M.[18]

The plane that hit the Pentagon, the world's largest building, penetrated three of the structure's five concentric rings. It entered the southwest wall that faces Arlington National Cemetery. At the time of the crash, many of the more than twenty thousand civilian and military Pentagon workers were huddled around television sets watching reports of the suicide mission just carried out at the World Trade Center in New York.

Although 189 innocent lives were lost at the Pentagon, it could have been much, much worse. By chance, the airliner hit one of the least occupied sections of the building. The plane struck close to the helicopter landing area and near a section of building where extensive renovation was taking place. Work had been recently completed in the part of the Pentagon known as "wedge one," but only a few employees had moved back into it. The adjacent "wedge two" was being prepared for renovation and was virtually empty when the plane slammed into the building.

It has been widely reported that the ultimate target of hijacked United flight 93, which crashed in Pennsylvania, was either the U.S. Capitol or the White House. In fact, the fourth passenger jet to crash during the September 11 attacks may have been destined to fly into a nuclear power plant to cause a Chernobyl-type disaster. In the months following the attacks, the FBI revealed a report that the four terrorists who seized the plane may have been attempting to steer it toward a cluster of nuclear power stations on the East Coast. The most likely target was Three Mile Island, near Harrisburg, Pennsylvania, site of America's most serious nuclear accident in 1979. United flight 93 crashed into a field near the tiny town of Shanksville, ninety minutes after taking off from Newark. All forty-four passengers and crew on board died.[19]

British intelligence sources reported a week before the attacks that the FBI sent a report to them saying a "credible source" had said terrorists might have been planning to hit a nuclear plant. Had it breached the plant's reactor vessel, such a strike could have caused an incident on the scale of the Chernobyl disaster in Ukraine, which spread radioactive material over thousands of square miles in 1986. Sources said that Three Mile Island, which is partly owned by British Energy, was the subject of surveillance by some of the hijackers and their associates in the months before the terrorist attacks. One security official said, "Early on in the investigation we did receive a report from the FBI that the plane may have been heading for a nuclear power station. This was based on their analysis that Pittsburgh is near several power stations. There is some plausibility to this and we're not trying to dismiss it. But it may well be that nobody will ever know where the plane was going."[20]

Engineering experts are divided over whether concrete containment shields around nuclear power stations could withstand a direct hit from a large passenger aircraft, especially one carrying two hundred thousand pounds of fuel, enough for flight 93 to reach its destination of San Francisco. The containment buildings at a nuclear facility generally have an outer structure, a three-foot-thick concrete dome containing large amounts of reinforced steel. Inside is a steel "lining" one inch by four inches thick. There are usually two more concrete walls close to the reactor, each one foot thick and reinforced with steel bars. But these walls do not enclose the top of the reactor completely. The reactor vessel itself is about four inches by six inches thick and made of high-carbon steel.

All reactors are designed to withstand impact by a light plane. Experts say it is unclear whether a larger modern jet loaded with fuel, deliberately flown at high speed, could break open the reactor vessel. Still, it is known the resultant fire could, however, cause enough damage to allow radioactive material into the air.[21]

The drama aboard flight 93 as a small group of passengers tried to seize control of the plane from the hijackers during its final few minutes has become an emblem of American heroism during the events of September 11. Delayed forty minutes in taking off from Newark's congested airport, the plane was in the early stages of its journey when its passengers started hearing that other aircraft had been hijacked and at least one had flown into the twin towers of the World Trade Center.

Todd Beamer, one of the passengers, called an emergency operator on an onboard telephone after he and fellow passengers learned of the first attack. He explained that flight 93 had also been hijacked. He said there were three hijackers—two with knives and one with what he thought was a bomb strapped to his waist. In fact, there were four, and by this time the fourth was almost certainly flying the plane.

Beamer, who was married with two young sons and another baby on the way, told the operator: "We're going to do something. I know I'm not going to get out of this." He explained that some of passengers had decided to jump on the terrorist thought to have the bomb. With the telephone left on, he could be heard saying: "Are you guys ready? Let's roll." The operator heard screams and a few minutes later the line went dead.

Immediately after 9/11, the FBI and other law enforcement

agencies spread out looking for what might have been the fifth team of hijackers, as was reported from Russian intelligence weeks before the attacks. Suicide hijackers may have also been on board American Airlines flight 43 from Boston, which was grounded due to a mechanical problem. The plane had been scheduled to take off at 8:10 A.M., just twenty-five minutes after American Airlines flight 11, which struck the World Trade Center.

It was revealed that the FBI was also "very interested" in people whose names appeared on the passenger lists of several other flights that were in the air when the first attacks occurred. Those planes were then prematurely landed under the orders of air traffic controllers in response to the attacks on the World Trade Center and the Pentagon. None of the passengers being sought by the FBI reappeared to board the same, rescheduled flights when the grounding order on commercial planes in the U.S. was lifted on September 14. Another might have been a United Airlines flight, scheduled to leave Kennedy International Airport from New York to San Francisco. When the plane was grounded because of the attacks, four men described as "Middle Eastern–looking" refused to return to their seats and hurriedly left as soon as its doors opened. They were never found or questioned.

## The Economic Impact

Beyond the psychological and human toll the 9/11 attacks wrought, the direct and indirect economic losses also were immense. Although studies are currently underway to measure the impact of the attacks on the U.S. economy, at the time of this writing, no comprehensive report has been completed. Nevertheless, it doesn't take an economist to see the consequences of 9/11.

For example, although the U.S. economy was already sliding toward recession before the attacks, the number of jobs lost in the four months immediately following the attacks was about the same number of total layoffs—1.1 million—in the eight months prior to 9/11.

## Immediate Layoffs by Sector[22]

| Sector | Announced 9/12/01–1/21/02 |
|---|---|
| Transportation | 139,215 |
| Hospitality, Tourism, Entertainment | 139,840 |
| Communications and Utilities | 132,096 |
| Manufacturing | 426,948 |
| Retail Trade | 45,706 |
| Services | 50,530 |
| Finance, Insurance, and Real Estate | 67,735 |
| Public Administration | 48,343 |
| Other | 4,240 |
| **Total** | **1,054,653** |

Direct economic costs from the attacks included:

Human loss
Property loss (buildings, airliners, vehicles, utilities)
Response costs (debris removal, clean up)
Health effects (injuries and emotional distress)
Insurance claims
Legal fees

Indirect economic costs included:

Lost employee income
Lost business profits
Spending reductions
Fiscal impacts such as reduced tax revenues

Beyond direct and indirect losses, the economic effects of the War on Terrorism, launched by the United States as a direct result of the attacks, has not yet been determined. Public statements by the Bush administration have assured the world and the American people that U.S. action in Afghanistan will not be the only steps taken to combat global terrorism. Further, the impact of increased governmental spending to combat terrorism at home—including the federalization of aviation security and the creation of a Homeland Security Department—will reshape the role and responsibility of the federal government.

The measurable economic effects of 9/11 will most certainly be into the hundreds of billions of dollars. And, when combined with the psychological and human impact, the effects of the assault will continue to influence our society for decades to come.

## GLARING WEAKNESSES WITHIN THE AVIATION SECURITY SYSTEM

Commercial aviation was used in the 9/11 attacks precisely because of specific defects that existed within the security system. These failings, many of which have received little or no attention at all, literally and figuratively opened the door for the terrorists to wreak extraordinary damage. Like the intelligence community, aviation security officials ignored the warning signs. They were plain to see, no question about it. Yet despite red flags flying everywhere, those entrusted to run aviation security in this country prior to 9/11 dropped the ball.

We have learned since then that the 9/11 hijackers were casing airports in the weeks prior to the attacks and taking test runs on flights to better pinpoint the weaknesses within the system. Law enforcement officials suggest that the evidence reveals "the hijackers were quiet, studious, calculating, and thorough" in their operation and did their research without raising suspicion.[23] In a speech in early May 2002, FBI Director Mueller echoed those comments when he said, "The September 11 terrorists spent a great deal of time and effort figuring out how America works. They knew the ins and outs of our systems."

Although it is believed the hijackers took several flights between 1999 and September 11, 2001, the FBI has nailed down twelve flights that the terrorists took immediately prior to the attacks. The FBI believes the terrorists focused on transcontinental flights with lots of fuel, so they could turn the planes into flying weapons of mass destruction. Testimony from passengers and flight crews reveal that the hijackers took pictures of the cockpit door and appeared to take notes during flights in May, June, July, and August of 2001.[24]

Janice Shineman, who was traveling through Boston's Logan Airport on September 9, reported to the FBI after the attacks that she observed Mohammed Atta, the alleged ringleader of the 9/11 hijackers, casing the terminal where American Airlines flight 11 was boarded. "He had no briefcase, no luggage. I remember telling my limo driver, 'That man has no business here,' " said Shineman, who first spotted Atta as she stepped out of a limousine at the American Airlines gate the morning of her flight to California.[25] Shineman added that she watched the fierce-looking Atta take copious notes on a note card "in what looked like Arabic." He then placed the notes into a red envelope.[26]

Given that the 9/11 hijackers were searching and probing for weaknesses in the aviation security regimen, it is incumbent for us to understand what they may have seen and learned. Doing so will give us better insight into what might have actually happened on the flights and why, and illustrate many of the vulnerabilities in aviation security that allowed these terrible events to occur. This way we can prevent similar calamities from happening in the future.

## Ease of Getting into the Cockpit

None of the 9/11 flights had the captain or copilot telling air traffic controllers that they were being hijacked. It is therefore logical to assume that the terrorists overtook the cockpits in one of the following manners: either by stealth; sudden and brute force; or, creating a disturbance in the aircraft that would have compelled one of the flight deck members to exit the cockpit to de-escalate the situation and exposing the flight deck to penetration by the hijackers. Remember, had the 9/11 terrorists not been able to get into the cockpit of the airliners, they wouldn't have been able to turn the plane into a flying missile and inflict the damage on the ground that they did.

### Taking the Cockpit by Stealth

On at least two of the hijacked flights of September 11, communications revealed that flight attendants had been stabbed and killed prior to the crashes. On American flight 11, the first to career into the World Trade Center, flight attendant Betty Ong called the American reservations desk from a seatback phone. "She said two flight attendants had been stabbed, one was on oxygen," said the manager on duty.[27] On United flight 175, the second plane to fly into the WTC, the airline reported that one flight attendant had been stabbed and two crewmembers had been killed.[28] The most likely reason for the assaults on the flight attendants was to obtain their key to the cockpit door, which they each carried in compliance with FAA regulations. We can assume, therefore, that the terrorists were able to unlock the doors and literally walk into the cockpits.

FAA Order Number 8400.10, dated January 7, 1997, responded to a National Transportation Safety Board recommendation that had asked the FAA to require each flight attendant to have a cockpit key in his/her possession at all times while on duty. Remarkably, this is what the order said, in the FAA's own words:

> During a recent accident, the pilots received information that they had an engine fire when the right engine fire warning light illuminated. . . . Because of the need for a flight attendant to retrieve a cockpit key from its assigned storage area before being able to unlock the cockpit door. . . . The Safety Board is concerned that having only one cockpit key available and stored in a pre-

arranged area may not allow a key to be readily accessible to all flight attendants in an emergency. Therefore, the Safety Board believes that the FAA should require that each flight attendant have a cockpit key in his/her possession at all times, while on duty.

To justify their decision, the Safety Board cited Title 14 of the Code of Federal Regulations (14 CFR) part 121, section 121.313 (g). It stipulated that there must be a key for each door that separates a passenger compartment from another compartment that has emergency exit provisions. The key must be readily available for each crewmember. In addition, 14 CFR part 121, section 121.587, stipulates that the cockpit door must be locked during flight. "Therefore, air carriers should ensure that each flight attendant has a cockpit key in his/her possession during the performance of duties in flight."[29]

### Taking the Cockpit by Sudden and Brute Force

In the twenty-four months prior to September 11, 2001, some thirty cases were recorded of passengers either completely or partially entering the cockpit of a commercial carrier. In one of the more publicized cases, on a Southwest Airlines flight from Las Vegas to Salt Lake City in August 2000, a nineteen-year-old passenger rushed and entered the cockpit twice before other passengers subdued him. He eventually died from suffocation and his death was ruled a homicide. Nevertheless, the U.S. Attorney in Salt Lake City did not file charges against the passengers because he felt there was no criminal conduct involved.[30]

On March 16, 2000, during an Alaska Airlines flight from Puerta Vallarta, Mexico, to San Francisco, a male passenger began babbling incoherently, wandering from seat to seat, and stripping off his clothes. His agitation increased, passengers said, until he broke into the cockpit, threatened to kill the pilot, and grabbed for the controls. The pilot momentarily lost control of the jet as the copilot fended off the six-foot-two, 250-pound intruder with an ax. Some of the forty-one passengers aboard tackled and eventually restrained him.

In one of the more frightening cockpit intrusions, in December 2000 a deranged passenger entered the cockpit of a British Airways jumbo jet traveling from London to Nairobi and grabbed the controls, sending the plane plummeting toward the ground before the crew regained control. According to statements from passengers and crew, the man, after barging into the cockpit, disengaged the autopilot, and sent the plane hurtling into a ten-thousand-foot dive. The crew struggled with the man, sending the plane into a second dive before the crew finally recovered command of the aircraft.

Many of the 379 passengers aboard the Boeing 747-400 screamed and prayed as they were jolted out of their early morning slumber and found hysteria sweeping the cabin. For more than two minutes, passengers believed they were going to die as the plane continued to plummet. Finally, after what must have seemed like an eternity, the man was overpowered by passengers in the first-class section and the flight crew.

During the melee, the intruder bit the ear of the captain and injured four other passengers and a crewmember. The first officer was eventually able to get the man out of the cockpit while the reserve officer was able to fly the aircraft. Aviation experts believe that had the incident raged on for another four or five seconds, the copilot would not have been able to regain control of the plane because the aircraft was nearly on its back. The results of the medical examinations conducted on the passenger showed that the twenty-seven-year-old Kenyan was mentally disturbed. Passengers said they saw the perpetrator wandering around one section of the plane for about thirty minutes before he made his way toward the cockpit and burst in, lunging for the controls.[32]

One hour into a February 2001 flight from Miami to New York, a young couple sitting in coach class calmly asked the flight attendant if they could move into the two empty seats in the first-class section because, "They believed the elderly woman sitting in the aisle next them was trying to kill them." The attendant, believing they were joking, politely said "No" and continued serving drinks. At this point, a seemingly normal trip became a near-disaster. The girlfriend, incredulous that she was denied an upgrade, became enraged. Screaming obscenities at the top of her lungs, she jumped up from her seat and made a mad dash, on her knees, for first class.

Following his girlfriend's lead, the man stood up and announced to everyone that the overhead compartments were filled with machine guns and that she was carrying a bomb. As his girlfriend continued to run toward the front of the plane, the boyfriend grabbed two coffeepots and yelled, "These are my weapons!" as he threw coffee on a flight attendant and burned her. Reaching first class, the man kicked a hole in the cockpit door and the woman grabbed the emergency exit handle shouting, "We're taking this plane down!" Fortunately, four male passengers tackled the boyfriend before he could do anything else, beating him unconscious, while two other flight attendants subdued the woman and then sat on her until the flight could be diverted to Atlanta. Upon arrival, the two were sent to a hospital for observation. They were released after it was discovered that they were both under psychiatric evaluation in their hometown. Their family doctor had ordered them to take their medication and stay within five miles of their residence. Unfortunately, they'd had the urge to travel and had acted upon it.[33]

Whether drunk, mentally ill, or under the influence of narcotics, disruptive passengers educated the 9/11 hijackers about how easy it was to storm the cockpit of an aircraft. Imagine how simple it could have been for four or five well-motivated and calculating terrorists to get in. And, despite the heightened security measures following 9/11, seven incidents involving disruptive passengers completely or partially entering a cockpit took place in the six months *after* the attacks.

These cockpit intrusions would not have been possible, however, had the structure of the door been reinforced. Instead, to insure easy egress from the flight deck in the case of an emergency, cockpit doors were designed to be weak. A normal-sized man with a karate kick or a shoulder shove could have broken down a 9/11 cockpit door without too much exertion. Because of the cost to the airlines of reinforcing the cockpit doors of eight thousand commercial airliners, the FAA failed to do anything about the problem.

As an example of further reluctance to address these issues, in hearings to improve the airlines on Capitol Hill in early 2001, Sen. John McCain and other lawmakers instead stressed the problems of delayed and missed flights, and lost baggage. They largely overlooked security problems, even though FAA agents, consumer groups, and flight attendants had clamored for years for stronger cockpit doors that were implemented only after 9/11.

### Taking the Cockpit by Creating a Disturbance

The failure on the part of the FAA to effectively deal with the air rage problem prior to 9/11 allowed the terrorists another path into the cockpits of the airliners. My first book in the study of aviation security dealt with this very real threat. While I have no intention of restating all the findings of that book here, it is without question that the issue played a principal role in the execution of the terrorist attacks.

For ten years prior to 9/11, not a single commercial aircraft was hijacked in the United States. For nearly a generation, disturbances perpetrated by disruptive passengers were widely viewed as the greatest threat to cabin security. In calendar year 2000, for example, internal FAA research revealed that more than ten thousand cases of "air rage"—an abusive, abnormal, or aberrant act—took place. Nevertheless, despite the scope and magnitude of the problem, nothing of consequence was ever done. In 2000, only 266 cases of disruptive behavior, less than 3 percent of all incidents, were ever prosecuted.

After United flight 175 was hijacked, the dispatcher at United's operations center in Chicago, who had been assigned to follow both flights 175 and 93 as well as fourteen other planes, sent an electronic text message to the airliners that read, "Beware, cockpit intrusion."[34] On the morning of September 11, 2001, such a message would most likely have been interpreted by the pilot of a domestic flight as an air rage incident, not a hijacking. On United flight 93, the last of the four planes to be hijacked, the pilots received the message and typed a one-word reply: "Confirmed." The plane was taken over by four terrorists a few minutes later.[35]

Although the FAA wasn't doing anything to address the rising tide of air rage, airlines had formulated policies that created glaring security vulnerabilities. In the event of a disruptive incident in the cabin that appeared to be escalating, pilots were encouraged by the airlines to intervene personally to take care of the situation. Rather than divert the flight to the nearest airport where law enforcement officials could handle the situation, pilots were instructed to exit the cockpit and confront the disruptive passenger head on.

## Lax Screening Protocols

Incredibly, nine of the hijackers were selected for special security screenings the morning of 9/11. Six were chosen for extra security by a computerized screening system; two others were singled out because of irregularities with their documents; and one was listed on ticket documents as the travel companion to one who had questionable identification.[36] Yet, in the end, they were all allowed to later board their flights.

On 9/11, according to FAA security protocols, passengers selected for further evaluation were only to have their *checked* luggage further swept for explosives or unauthorized weapons. The passengers' carry-on bags and their person were not to be more fully examined. And, as only a couple of the terrorists actually had checked bags, there was no security protocol in place to detect the box cutters and other possible weapons they were carrying with them. Had a security protocol requiring more intensive examination of *all* luggage—both carry-ons and checked bags—as well as the clothing of a selected passenger existed, it is more than likely that the discovery of several young Arab men carrying box cutters with one-way, first-class tickets purchased with cash would have thrown up a red flag. Unfortunately, we'll never know.

Screening deficiencies, particularly at Boston's Logan from where flights 11 and 175 departed, were most evident for years. Between 1997 and 2000, undercover FAA inspectors found that Logan security employees routinely failed to detect test items like pipe bombs and guns. To further make the point, Brian Sullivan, a former FAA special agent for ten years who retired in January 2001, arranged to have a local television investigative reporter work with a former member of the FAA's elite Red Team to conduct security assessments at Logan. "We were successful in penetrating the security screening points at Logan eleven out of twelve times," said Sullivan. "And if we were successful at doing it, potential terrorists could as well."[37] Even more disheartening, the weapons the terrorists used—box cutters in particular—were permitted under the existing FAA security regimen.

The neglect to properly assess the threat of suicidal hijackers and shore up the vulnerabilities that existed within the aviation security system enabled the terrorists to overwhelmingly succeed in inflicting a great deal of damage on the United States. From those failures emerged a supposedly new way of conducting aviation security in this country. The remainder of this book will analyze the creation and implementation of that new aviation security system, which was born out of the tragedies of September 11, 2001.

# CHAPTER 2

# THE CULTURE
# OF COMPROMISE

"No accountability, no justice, no progress."

—Anonymous

To get a true sense of where the aviation security regimen is headed, we need to first take a step back and look at how the system evolved over the past decades up to September 11, 2001. Then, once we understand where aviation security has come from, we can better undertake an assessment of the system we presently have. And, finally, we can then look at what the future holds. Disheartening, however, the history of aviation security in the United States isn't very uplifting.

As the use of commercial aviation in the United States increased exponentially throughout the second half of the twentieth century, the roles and responsibilities of the FAA as the industry's regulatory agency expanded proportionately. Prior to 1958, two separate federal agencies worked on behalf of the federal government to regulate commercial aviation. The Civil Aeronautics Administration (CAA) was responsible for air traffic control, airman and aircraft certification, safety enforcement, and airway development. The Civil Aeronautics Board (CAB) was entrusted with safety rule making, accident investigation, and economic regulation of the airlines. With the introduction of jetliners and the burgeoning growth of the industry in the 1950s, Congress sought to place all of the federal government's regulatory authority in the hands of a single agency.

The Federal Aviation Act of 1958 transferred the CAA's and CAB's functions to a new independent agency—the Federal Aviation Agency. In addition, however—and this is a big one—Congress gave the new agency another mandate: to advance the expansion of the civil aviation industry. The legislation was summarized as such:

> An act to continue the Civil Aeronautics Board as an agency of the United States to create a Federal Aviation Agency, to provide for the *regulation and promotion* of civil aviation in such a manner as to best foster its development and safety.[1]

In Title III of the bill, Section 305, the FAA's responsibility to support air commerce was further defined:

> The Administrator is empowered and directed to *encourage and foster* the development of civil aeronautics and air commerce in the United States and abroad.

Throughout its existence, the FAA would come to be defined as a federal agency that was torn apart by two competing and divergent goals. How can it nurture both market forces and public safety at the same time? A formidable, if not almost impossible, task, to be sure.

Asking a federal agency to regulate an industry it is also charged with promoting creates a basic conflict of interest and raises more questions than answers. Moreover, Congress never gave any parameters to the FAA to help the agency recognize where the line of promotion ended and where the line of regulation began. The agency was left to determine for itself the ways in which it worked with the industry. Ultimately, as a result of the conflicting Congressional imperatives, a regulatory body would emerge that would be first confused and then snarled by its own mission.

# MARKET FORCES COME TO DOMINATE THE FAA

As the aviation industry became more and more critical to the well-being of the U.S. economy, commercial interests began to take precedence over other concerns. Starting in the late 1960s, when the Federal Aviation Agency was moved from the Commerce Department to the newly created Department of Transportation and became the Federal Aviation Administration, the airlines, through intensive lobbying efforts on Capitol Hill, strove to insure that their ultimate objectives were met. These objectives were more often in line with the "promotional" and commercial aspects of the FAA's mission but were contrary to the safety and security mandates of the agency.

When it came to aviation security, and in particular the FAA's role in it prior to September 11, 2001, we find one of those situations where the balance between government regulation and the desire for profits got way out of whack. In short, market forces ran rampant throughout the agency for decades and eventually marginalized the FAA and its security functions. Again and again, policy decisions and solutions that should have been made by the FAA were deferred by the agency to the airlines or to Congress. Over time, the assigned regulator (FAA) came to be regulated by the market regulatee (the airlines). In essence, the tail wagged the dog.

Under Title XII Security Provisions, Section 1201 of the Federal Aviation Act of 1958, the role of the FAA with regard to security was described as follows:

> The purpose of this title is to establish security provisions which will encourage and permit the maximum use of the navigable airspace by civil aircraft consistent with the national security.

At that moment in time, aviation security in the United States was still in its infancy. Little or no research had been done in the field and government's role was minor at best. Over the next forty-plus years, as commercial air travel expanded, aviation security evolved along with it. Until the terrorist attacks of September 11, 2001, civil aviation security was a combination of laws, regulations, and resources. The program was supposed to be a system of shared and complementary responsibilities involving the federal government, air carriers, passengers, and airports. In theory, the FAA set the standards and guidelines, and air carriers and airports implemented them. And, if the guidelines and standards were not being followed by the carriers, the FAA was mandated to enforce the existing regimen. Passengers and the users of air cargo services, who were the ultimate beneficiaries of the program, paid for aviation security through surcharges included in the price of airline tickets and cargo shipments.[2]

## Theoretical Roles and Responsibilities of the Pre 9/11 Aviation Security System

| FAA | Airlines | Airports |
|---|---|---|
| Make policy | Screen passengers | Protect air operations |
| Identify and assess threats | Screen baggage | Provide access control |
| Approve security plans | Screen cargo | Provide law enforcement |
| Inspect compliance | Guard aircraft | Dispose of explosives |
| | | Provide direction |
| | | Initiate necessary changes |

And, although authority might be delegated or shared (i.e., a private security company might operate the security checkpoints), the ultimate responsibility for the safety and security of civil aviation was to rest with the FAA.[3]

As time went on, it became clear that Congress had made a grievous error when it gave the agency the job of commercially promoting the same industry it was charged with regulating. It was frankly a bad idea. The "Dual Mandate," as it came to be called, was, more than anything else, to define and shape the mission, goals, and actions of the FAA. Moreover, it would eventually lead the agency, at the public expense, into a position that allowed a culture of compromise to fester.

In 1996, in response to the obvious long-term negative results stemming from the Dual Mandate, Congress created new legislation that eliminated some of the language from the original 1958 bill. The FAA Reauthorization Act under Title IV eliminated the word "promotion" and inserted in its place "assigning, maintaining, and enhancing safety and security as the highest priorities in air commerce." Surely, Congress knew all wasn't well with the FAA to have made this adjustment in language. Yet, despite the change in the mission of the FAA, the dysfunctional culture remained. The airlines continued to press their interests and the FAA, for the most part, deferred.

## A Great Job Lobbying

To understand how market forces usurped the regulatory authority of the FAA, when it came to aviation security on and before 9/11, we need only to look at who was working on behalf of the airlines and how much was spent to buy influence. Doing so reveals the scope of the airlines' reach into the FAA when it came to determining aviation security policy. It also reveals the extent to which the agency had become beholden to the industry it was supposed to be regulating.

Individuals or groups promoting special interests are as old as America itself. James Madison, in *Federalist #10*, recognized that particular factions within society would always seek to advance their interests at the expense of others:

Liberty is to faction what air is to fire, a liment without which it instantly expires. But it could not be a less folly to abolish liberty, which is essential to political life, because it nourishes faction than it would be to wish the annihilation of air, which is essential to animal life, because it imparts to fire its destructive agency.

Madison, like most of the Founding Fathers, believed that the limited and separated structure of the government they designed would naturally win out against those who wanted an activist one. However, Madison and many of his cohorts were wrong. What they failed to envision were the ways politicians, bureaucrats, and commercial interests could manipulate the government to easily advance the desires of the few over those of the many. Naturally gridlocked, decentralized, divided, and weak government—the foundations of the Constitution—were in due time overcome by the energies of activism and centralization.

The efforts of the airline industry and the people who left government to influence policy decisions on its behalf are a striking example of what determined, well-connected, and well-financed lobbying can do. In getting their way, the airlines showed they were much more successful at it than almost anybody else. When confronted with the tough decision of siding with public safety or aligning themselves with market forces, the FAA most often chose to support the airlines, even when it flew in the face of logic and sound public policy.

Market forces will always seek to dominate regulatory authority, a reality not exclusively endemic to commercial aviation. Whatever the enterprise, uncontrolled and unrestrained market forces will inevitably work toward commercial outcomes alone. Whether it is in aviation, finance, chemicals, medicine, automobiles, or fabricating widgets, the drive for profits will always overshadow every other interest, including the public good. And, while the desire for profits allows talent, opportunity, and creativity to flourish, unregulated market forces in due time will swallow up everything else around them. This is the nature of unbridled capitalism at its core.

As someone who has lived abroad, traveled to more than 120 countries, and conducted business all over the world, the author believes that one of the greatest assets of the United States is its system of market forces coexisting with the government's regulatory authority. Better than anywhere else on the planet, the economic interests of the marketplace and the protection of the public good have, for the most part, gotten along pretty well. Most countries fail to ever come close to striking this critical balance. They tend to favor one over the other. Too much dependency on government authority squashes entrepreneurship, innovation, and growth. On the other hand, an overemphasis on the commercial side leads to uncontrolled corruption, instability, and inequality.

Of course there are times in the United States when government has crossed the line and overreached its power. The scourge of McCarthyism in the 1950s serves as a stark reminder of how government authority can go way over the line. There also have been moments in our history when business has been allowed to run roughshod over the well-being of the American people. The recent spate of accounting frauds on the part of some our nation's largest corporations has led to a crisis of confidence for many about the real benefits of the free market. But, generally speaking, government and the free market have done a decent job of working together to better the American way of life. Not always. But certainly better than any other country.

The linchpin in this difficult balancing act is the character of the individuals and organizations that operate within governmental agencies. Regulatory authority is only able to function effectively when civil servants, entrusted and paid by the people to guard the public interest, successfully ward off special interests and the formidable power of market forces. A breakdown at this level assures that commercial interests will penetrate and eventually jeopardize an agency's integrity. If market forces are permitted to move about unabated, the agency—and our country—will eventually become compromised.

The cadre of lobbyists working for major U.S. airlines have worked in the highest levels of government and read like a Who's Who list of Washington insiders. Just a few noteworthy names include:[4]

| Individual | Past Employment | Lobbied For |
| --- | --- | --- |
| Linda Daschle | FAA Deputy Administrator | American |
| George Mitchell | Senate Majority Leader, 1989–1995 | Northwest |
| Ken Duberstein | Chief of Staff to Ronald Reagan | Northwest |
| Bob Packwood | Republican Senator, 1969–1995 | United |
| Wendell Ford | Democratic Senator, 1974–1998 | Delta |
| Harold Ickes | Deputy Chief of Staff to Bill Clinton | United |
| William Coleman | Secretary, DOT, Ford administration | US Airways |
| Patrick Murphy | Deputy Assistant Secretary, DOT | Northwest |
| William Ris Jr. | Counsel, Senate Aviation Subcommittee | Continental |
| Mark Gerchick | Deputy Assistant Secretary, DOT | Northwest |

The activities of Linda Daschle alone provide a typical example of how ex-government officials and the airline industry opened the door for market forces to overtake the FAA. As wife of the current senate minority leader and the former deputy administrator of the FAA, Daschle includes among her many clients American Airlines, which has had seven fatal crashes since 1994 (not including the World Trade center flights). The airline has incurred millions of dollars in federal fines for a host of safety violations, and its employees have been caught in embarrassing drug smuggling stings. Even as its planes crashed, American Airlines used Daschle to lobby to consistently water down security regulations that might have helped to foil the World Trade Center attacks, such as instituting reinforced cockpit doors and stricter guidelines at security checkpoints.[5]

Before 9/11, the FAA was pressured by Congress to go easy on airlines and airports for security lapses, because Congress itself was pressured by lobbyists like Daschle and others who represent airlines focused on profits and not "inconveniences" like security. What emerged was a system that resembled cotton candy: 90 percent sugar and 10 percent air. When, for example, a checkpoint screener would fail to discover an FAA-approved test object put through by an FAA special agent, the airline would occasionally receive a fine. These fines would accumulate over a period of months or years and finally be negotiated down to pennies on the dollar at special administrative hearings in Washington or other regional FAA offices. The screening company that was contracted by the airline would be instructed to fire the offending worker. In most cases, the worker would be rehired shortly thereafter. The blame for the breach would be fixed on the FAA's poor security standards and the screening company's lack of enforcement. The airlines skated every time. And it was the industry's lobbyists who made sure this pattern was allowed to continue.[6]

In 1990, in the wake of the Pan Am flight 103 explosion over Lockerbie, Scotland, a Presidential Commission on Aviation Security and Terrorism was ordered by the elder President Bush. It concluded its report by saying:

> The U.S. civil aviation security system is seriously flawed and has failed to provide the proper level of protection for the traveling public. This system needs major reform. Rhetoric is no substitute for strong, effective action.

As a result of the commission's findings, a few brave Congressmen sought to impose a ten-year criminal background check on all employees at the nation's airports. This measure was strongly opposed by the airlines on the grounds it wasn't necessary and it would raise security costs to the point that it would ultimately increase passenger fares and hurt the industry.

To help its efforts fighting the measure, the airlines hired former CIA and FBI Director William Webster to lobby Capitol Hill. The ultimate outcome, which came six years later after numerous delays, was a watered-down version of the original legislation that created few, if any, substantive security improvements. For example, existing airport employees were exempted from the new law.[7]

Standing behind Daschle, Webster, and the dozens of other heavy hitters lobbying the government on behalf of the airlines was a substantial war chest. In 2000 alone, the air transport industry spent $46,020,819 on lobbyists. Some of the biggest spenders that year were:[8]

| Organization | Amount |
|---|---|
| Air Transport Association | $1,180,000 |
| American Airlines | $2,400,000 |
| Delta Airlines | $2,340,000 |
| Northwest Airlines | $2,620,000 |
| United Airlines | $3,240,000 |
| US Airways | $1,340,000 |

Beyond spending millions on lobbying, the airline industry invested substantial sums in donations to elected officials from the industry. For years, the airlines were some of the most generous contributors to both political parties on Capitol Hill.[9]

## 2000 Election Cycle

| Organization | Total Amount | Given to Democrats | Given to Republicans |
|---|---|---|---|
| American Airlines | $1,417,447 | 41% | 59% |
| Northwest Airlines | $1,367,705 | 53% | 47% |
| United Airlines | $886,153 | 37% | 63% |
| Delta Airlines | $592,311 | 50% | 50% |
| Continental Airlines | $446,984 | 25% | 75% |

# 1998 Election Cycle

| Organization | Total Amount | Given to Democrats | Given to Republicans |
|---|---|---|---|
| American Airlines | $932,681 | 40% | 60% |
| Northwest Airlines | $861,496 | 45% | 55% |
| United Airlines | $593,771 | 53% | 47% |
| Delta Airlines | $392,927 | 30% | 70% |
| Continental Airlines | $242,052 | 45% | 55% |

## The Gore Commission

An example of how the FAA had its power expropriated by the airline industry via Congressional pressure was the manner in which the industry reacted to the recommendations made by the Gore Commission. On July 25, 1996, shortly after the crash of TWA flight 800, President Bill Clinton asked Vice President Al Gore to chair a commission on improving air transportation safety and security.[10] As a result, the White House Commission on Aviation Safety and Security, commonly known as the Gore Commission, conducted an in-depth analysis of U.S. commercial airlines' safeguards against terrorist attacks. In its final report, the Gore Commission found that security measures used by U.S. airlines needed to be drastically improved, just like the previous federal commission had six years earlier.

> The federal government should consider aviation security as a national security issue, and provide substantial funding for capital improvements. The Commission believes that terrorist attacks on civil aviation are directed at the United States, and that there should be an ongoing federal commitment to reducing the threats that they pose.[11]

However, of the fifty recommendations made by the Commission, nearly all were eventually watered down, delayed, or simply never considered by the FAA. On September 5, 1996, the Commission announced its preliminary findings and recommendations at a press conference held by Vice President Gore. Almost immediately, the airlines began a vigorous lobbying campaign aimed at the White House. Two weeks later, Chairman Gore retreated from the preliminary report in a letter to Carol Hallett, president of the industry's trade group, the Air Transport Association.

> I want to make it very clear that it is not the intent of this administration or of the Commission to create a hardship for the air transportation industry.

Gore added that the FAA would develop "a draft test concept . . . in full partnership with representatives of the airline industry."[12]

The day after Gore's letter, according to research from the Center for Responsive Politics, TWA donated $40,000 to the Democratic National Committee. By the time of the presidential election six weeks later, other airlines had poured large donations into Democratic Party committees: $265,000 from American Airlines; $120,000 from Delta Airlines; $115,000 from United Airlines; $87,000 from Northwest Airlines. In all, the airlines gave the Democratic Party $585,000 in the election's closing weeks. Elaine Kamarck, the Gore aide who had worked with the commission, denied that there was any connection between the donations and the commission's decisions. "Everyone was giving us money," she said. "When you're winning, everyone gives."[13]

Public Citizen, a national public interest organization, analyzed several areas where the FAA's responses to the Gore Commission's proposals reflected the interests of the airlines over better security. Two of the most egregious examples involved the certification of screening companies and employment history, verification, and criminal history records checks of all airport and airline employees.[14]

The Gore Commission recommended several ways that the performance of airport screening companies could be improved, including establishing a national job grade structure for screeners, creating meaningful measures to reduce high turnover rates, rewarding screeners for good performance, and not hiring screening companies on the sole basis of being the lowest bidder. The airlines objected to the recommendations on the predictable grounds that it would increase administrative costs significantly. The response from the FAA, in the form of a proposed rule, was to maintain the current system of allowing cost, not performance, to be the final determinant as to which screening company would be used by the airlines.

The Gore Commission also endorsed conducting criminal background checks of all airport and airline employees and went so far as to suggest the FBI conduct the investigations. In a May 19, 1997, letter, TWA argued that the background checks for their existing employees would only create administrative and financial burdens.

> These employees have had a five-year verification of their employment history. Their continued employment indicates that they have been good employees and do not pose a threat to aviation security. This proposed requirement would not do anything to increase aviation security. It would only add unnecessary costs and paperwork to the industry.[15]

Not surprisingly, the FAA ignored the Gore Commission's recommendation and nothing was ever done.

Even more disconcerting, several individuals who served on the Gore Commission doubted the genuineness of the recommendations and believed much of the exercise was merely a façade designed to keep market forces in control. One such person was Victoria Cummock, who had lost her husband John on Pan Am flight 103. After the final draft was produced, she stated in a letter to the vice president:

> I register my dissent with the final report. . . . Sadly, the overall emphasis of the recommendations reflects a clear commitment to the enhancement of aviation at the expense of the Commission's

mandate of enhancing aviation safety and security . . . I can not sign a report that blatantly allows the American flying public to be regularly placed at unnecessary risk.[16]

## Industry Control of Agency Advisory Committees

Since World War II, a rising trend among agencies within the executive branch of the federal government has been the increased dependence on advisory committees to formulate policy. When seeking to gather information or make decisions, agencies have increasingly gone outside of the federal government to seek advice, input, and expertise. As the system of advisory committees evolved, many people inside and outside of the government became concerned that the committees were representing only limited interests. To meet this concern, Congress enacted the Federal Advisory Committee Act (FACA) in 1972 (5 USC App. 1).

The legislation was designed to regulate the numerous committees, boards, commissions, councils, and similar groups that had been established. FACA originally set forth a series of rigid rules, procedures, and requirements that each advisory entity must follow if it is "established" or "utilized" by a federal agency. The act required agencies to follow specific procedures when creating advisory committees. The law also provided guidelines for the conduct of advisory committee activities.

One of the key provisions was for public participation within the committees. For example, the act stipulated that advisory committees hold open meetings by providing advance public notice. In addition, when creating an advisory committee, an agency must issue a charter approved by the General Services Administration and must select committee members in such a way as to assure that diverse views will be considered on the issues under review.

However, although the law was quite clear as to the make-up of the committee, over time industry representatives came to dominate FAA advisory committees. Take, for example, the members of the Aviation Security Advisory Committee in 2000:[17]

| Member | Organization |
| --- | --- |
| Michael Canavan | FAA, Committee Chair |
| Jan Brecht-Clark | FAA, Office of Civil Aviation Security Policy and Planning |
| Sharon Sharp | Department of Transportation |
| Deborah McElroy | Regional Airline Association |
| Paul Archambeault | Air Transport Association |
| Richard Mills | National Air Carriers Organization |
| Steve Alterman | Cargo Airline Association |
| Al Graser | American Association of Airport Executives |
| Warren Koppel | Airports Council International—North America |
| Steve Luckey | Airline Pilots Association |
| Bob Monetti | Victims of Pan Am 103 |
| Duane McGray | Airports Law Enforcement Agencies Network |
| Bob Martin | U.S. Postal Service |
| Bob Hutnick | INS |
| Beverly Wright | FBI |

A cursory look at the membership reveals that of the nine non-governmental representatives serving as members of the security committee, four represented airlines, two represented airports, and there was a single representative each for airline employees, local law enforcement, and passengers. So, in any debate, working group, or action undertaken by the committee, the airlines, along with their allies in the FAA and other federal agencies, held an automatic majority. The deck was already stacked in favor of the industry.

## THE CULTURE OF COMPROMISE

The broader outcome resulting from the minimalization of the FAA as a regulatory body was a disoriented, fragmented, and highly inefficient agency. A culture of compromise festered within the organization for years and came to permeate every level of it.

Although isolated pockets of dedicated employees existed throughout the FAA, the majority of the leadership throughout the agency's history had been devoted to making things as easy as possible for the airlines. Even on the rare occasion when the FAA pushed back, the airlines were almost always able to leverage their influence both inside and outside of the agency to get what they wanted. As a result, FAA security policy was treated more as a political issue than a mandated responsibility.

The intimate relationship between FAA management and the airlines may be best expressed in the fact that three of the more recent heads of the agency have come directly from the industry. David Hinson, who was in charge of the FAA from 1993 to 1996, was the founder and chief executive of Midway Airlines before joining the agency. The previously mentioned Linda Daschle worked for the Air Transport Association as a lobbyist before joining the FAA as deputy administrator from 1993 to 1996. She served briefly as the acting administrator in parts of 1996 and 1997. She is presently back lobbying for the airlines and for the company who is currently supplying the L-3 baggage screening machines to the Transportation Security Administration. In addition, T. Allan McArtor was a top executive at Federal Express before and after he served as FAA administrator from 1987 to 1989.

A Year 2000 Employee Attitude Survey of all FAA Civil Aviation Security (CAS) specialists revealed that a large percentage of the agency's front-line people felt largely detached and removed from what was going on at the higher levels (see table 1 on page 57). When asked whether they trusted FAA management, 56 percent said "no" and only 10 percent responded "yes." When queried if the FAA was good at identifying lessons learned, 58 percent of the agency's employees disagreed while only 21 percent agreed with the statement. When surveyed about whether the FAA was dedicated to reinventing itself in light of criticisms, 36 percent said it was not a priority while 14 percent agreed that it was a priority.

## Table 1. 2000 Employee Attitude Survey, FAA CAS Nation, March 2, 2001

| Survey Question | Strongly Disagree | Disagree | Neither | Agree | Strongly Agree |
|---|---|---|---|---|---|
| Promotions in my organization are given to those who are well qualified. | 30 | 28 | 19 | 17 | 6 |
| Recognition and rewards are based on merit. | 25 | 28 | 20 | 22 | 5 |
| Corrective actions are taken to deal with supervisors who perform poorly. | 39 | 25 | 22 | 12 | 2 |
| Supervisors are held accountable for achieving agency goals. | 13 | 15 | 25 | 35 | 12 |
| I trust FAA management. | 29 | 27 | 34 | 10 | 0 |
| My organization is good at identifying lessons learned. | 29 | 29 | 21 | 21 | 0 |
| My organization has made reinvention a priority. | 16 | 20 | 50 | 14 | 0 |

Responses to Selected Questions. Answers in %.

*Source:* FAA, Civil Aeromedical institute,
Human Resources Research Division, Omni International.

## A Red Team Member Steps Forward

Following the September 11 attacks, Bogdan Dzakovic, a former air marshal and member of the FAA's covert testing unit known as the Red Team, who is currently employed by the Transportation Security Administration, brought up several allegations regarding gross dereliction of duty by top FAA security officials. Created after the bombing of Pan Am flight 103 in 1988, the primary mission of the Red Team was to conduct covert security penetration testing for the purpose of identifying both localized and systemic vulnerabilities and to help strengthen FAA's regulatory inspection capabilities. Dzakovic joined the Red Team in 1995, having previously served as an air marshal since 1987.

The Red Team's covert testing was separate and apart from the day-to-day regulatory FAA oversight of airport/airline security. Red Team members were encouraged to "think out of the box" and come up with ever more creative ways to test the efficiency of the aviation security regimen. For example, standard FAA testing at security checkpoints would involve placing a simulated explosive device in an uncluttered bag, oriented in such a way that it would be easily identifiable to even the most poorly trained X-ray machine operator. Conversely, the Red Team would disguise the testing device within a cluttered bag.

Dzakovic claimed that while working for the Red Team, then FAA Associate Administrator for Civil Aviation Security Admiral Cathal Flynn suppressed testing results and directed the Red Team to not conduct follow-up inspections of airports that yielded especially poor testing results. This claim was backed up in a response to Dzakovic's allegations in a letter from Kenneth Mead, Inspector General for the Department of Transportation.

> Based on the "no rules" nature of the Red Team's testing techniques—which were more in line with actions that might be taken by terrorists and were not subject to the standardized FAA protocols—FAA held that Red Team findings were not suitable for civil enforcement proceedings.

In other words, the FAA would only make the airlines accountable for failures to detect easy-to-find explosives contained within the standard testing protocols. On the other hand, the inability to detect a more concealed explosive from the Red Team would be disregarded. The only motivation for the airlines was to catch the standard items so as to avoid a letter of reprimand or a fine. Red Team testing in essence meant nothing.

At Frankfurt Airport in Germany, where the bomb that destroyed Pan Am 103 was placed onboard via a piece of checked luggage, all Red Team testing in 1996, eight years later, resulted in failures. Because of the failures, FAA senior management ordered the Red Team testing at Frankfurt halted. In a letter from Cathal Flynn dated May 21, 1996, the appropriate German authorities were informed regarding the termination of the Red Team's work.

> The original intent was to complete approximately 60 assessments by March 1996. But, when there were no detections of the simulated IED in the test suitcases for the first 13 assessments, I elected to inform the U.S. carriers in Frankfurt of these results to see whether detection performance would improve. Testing resumed in March, but it is clear the results have not changed. Accordingly, I have decided now to conclude the project with our current total of 31 assessments.

The Red Team never returned to determine if the obvious problems were corrected at Frankfurt. During this time, it was becoming increasingly clear that a day like September 11, 2001, would not be a result of the failure of the system, but the result of a system designed to fail.

## Boston's Logan International: A Case Study in Compromise

It is no coincidence that the terrorists on 9/11 planned to hijack two planes—and quite possibly a third—on flights that originated from Logan Airport in Boston. For years, Logan was known throughout the industry as one of the least secure airports in the nation. From 1991 to 2000, Logan—the nation's eighteenth-busiest airport—had the fifth-highest number of security breaches. From 1997 through early 1999, there were at least 136 security violations at Logan, including easy access to parked planes and lax baggage inspections. In one of the more dramatic examples, a local teenager in 1999 was able to climb over an airport security fence, walk two miles across the tarmac, get through a jetway door that should have been locked, and travel as a stowaway on a British Airways 747 to London.[18]

As we now know, Mohammed Atta, the terrorists' ringleader, was also aware of Logan's shortcomings. He was seen casing the airport and studying its operations prior to the attacks. We may never fully understand whether a prohibited weapon like a firearm, pepper spray, or large knife were used along with legal weapons like box cutters on the flights that departed Logan on the morning of September 11, 2001. What is certain, however, is the relative ease with which illegal weapons were circumventing security checks at Logan and the ease of access to so-called secure areas at Logan before the attacks occurred.

Like that at airports across the country, the security at Logan was divided between the airport operator and the airlines, all under the final jurisdiction of the FAA. The Massachusetts Port Authority (Massport) ran the airport. After the stowaway incident of 1999, and probably as a result of increased scrutiny, citations for security violations by Massport ballooned to forty-two, more than any other airport authority in the United States. Of the forty-two violations at Logan, twenty-six were because a plainclothes agent was able to get onto the airfield, often by going through an alarmed door by either slipping behind someone already walking through or simply pushing the door open and triggering the alarm.[19] Massport was also cited for misplacing and losing keys to secure areas. It was later forced to rekey all the locks around the airport perimeter and institute a lock-and-key audit program.[20]

The security problems at Massport came on the heels of several scandals involving top officials within the organization. In August 1999, Massport Director Peter Blute was fired after it was revealed that he had participated in a publicly funded cruise on Boston Harbor that involved large amounts of alcohol, a Republican-party lobbyist, and several scantily clad women. The cruise culminated with one of the guests flashing her breasts at a *Boston Herald* photographer.[21] In June 2000, Massport's number-two security director, William J. Jaillet, quit after an internal investigation turned up evidence of sexual harassment. Interestingly enough, Jaillet had previously been a manager of the FAA's New England Region Civil Aviation Security Division, the government body charged with overseeing Massport.[22]

FAA management at Logan and throughout the New England region was inconsistent at best, incompetent at worst, and almost certainly compromised. In a decision that would eventually come back to haunt the agency, the FAA hired an admittedly inexperienced manager to supervise the Boston Civil Aviation Security Field Office (CASFO). In August 1998, Willie Gripper, then FAA's head of security for the New England region, selected Mary Carol Turano as manager of CASFO, which included both Logan and Providence's T. F Green Airport. In a memo to top officials at the agency, Gripper conceded that Turano had little or no experience in airport security:

> I recognize Mary Carol Turano does not currently have extensive program knowledge in air security issues, but I know she will be a quick learner.[23]

At the time Turano was selected, she had not yet begun the basic training that all FAA special agents must undergo. In fact, her previous experience within the FAA was as a budget analyst and national director of the agency's canine unit. After the 9/11 attacks, it was also revealed that Turano did not have a security badge that would have permitted her access to secure areas of the airport that she was overseeing.[24]

The morale at Logan among FAA security personnel during Turano's tenure reflected her detachment from the requirements of the position. In some respects, the FAA Civil Aviation Security (CAS) employees at Logan were more removed from the agency's

## Table 2. 2000 Employee Attitude Survey East Boston CASFO, March 2, 2001

| Survey Question | Strongly Disagree | Disagree | Neither | Agree | Strongly Agree |
|---|---|---|---|---|---|
| Promotions in my organization are given to those who are well qualified. | 18 | 28 | 27 | 18 | 9 |
| Recognition and rewards are based on merit. | 10 | 45 | 9 | 36 | 0 |
| Corrective actions are taken to deal with supervisors who perform poorly. | 73 | 9 | 0 | 18 | 0 |
| Supervisors are held accountable for achieving agency goals. | 0 | 36 | 37 | 9 | 18 |
| I trust FAA management. | 27 | 28 | 36 | 9 | 0 |
| My organization is good at identifying lessons learned. | 27 | 27 | 19 | 27 | 0 |
| My organization has made reinvention a priority. | 18 | 9 | 73 | 0 | 0 |

Responses to Selected Questions. Answers in %.

*Source:* FAA, Civil Aeromedical institute,
Human Resources Research Division, Omni International.

leaders and management than their counterparts across the country. (See tables 1 and 2) Logan's employees distrusted FAA management about as much as other CAS employees—54 percent to 56 percent. Both groups strongly felt the agency was poor at identifying lessons learned—54 percent at Logan, 58 percent nationwide. However, when it came to the competence of the managers at Logan, CAS employees there were much more frustrated than those at other airports across the country. Fully 82 percent of

Logan's FAA security personnel believed corrective actions were not taken to deal with supervisors who performed poorly, compared to 58 percent of all other CAS employees.

The problem of the airlines' unwillingness to securely run the checkpoints at Logan and to inspect checked baggage, and the FAA's reluctance to do anything about it, was raised before September 11, 2001, by several important people. In April, four months before the attacks, the public safety director at Massport, Joe Lawless, wrote a detailed memo urging Massport to prepare for a possible attack, citing reports that terrorists were operating in Boston. The memo, dated April 27, 2001, specifically warned that law enforcement in the Boston area had uncovered suspected terrorists, including some with links to the airport. Lawless later told the media, "I wrote it because I was concerned . . . because we had vulnerabilities that had to be addressed immediately."[25] In meetings earlier that month, Lawless suggested that Massport conduct their own criminal background checks on prospective employees. He believed two weaknesses within the airlines' security system were the lack of reporting by several police agencies to the airlines' databases and the lack of access to some records due to privacy reasons.[26]

Another critic of security at Logan was Brian Sullivan, a retired U.S. Army Military Police Lieutenant Colonel and former FAA Civil Aviation Security Specialist for the New England region. Sullivan, who left the FAA in January 2001, set out after his departure to expose what he called "the façade of aviation security that existed at Logan prior to the terrorist attacks."[27]

To prove his point, Sullivan contacted Deborah Sherman, an investigative reporter with WFXT television in Boston. In April of 2001, Sherman, with the help of Steve Elson, a retired FAA agent, conducted tests at Logan's screening checkpoints. On May 6, the broadcast aired and revealed that reporters were able to get items that should have been detected and resolved past screeners at Logan eleven out of twelve times. One such example was a knife six and three-quarters inches long that reporters were able to pass through in a belly pack and was never discovered. In addition, reporters were able to glean combinations to airport terminal doors, which gave them unfettered access to parked aircraft and cargo.

In what would come to be a prophetic letter to Massachusetts Senator John Kerry dated May 7, 2001, the day after the broadcast, Brian Sullivan wrote:

> With the concept of *Jihad*, do you think it would be difficult for a determined terrorist to get on a plane and destroy himself and all other passengers? Think what the result would be of a coordinated attack which took down several domestic flights on the same day. Considering the current threats, it is almost likely.[28]

Knowing what we know now about the culture of compromise that existed within the FAA, the agency's response to both Lawless's recommendations and the television investigation was almost predictable. In a May 21, 2001, letter, Michael Canavan, associate administrator of the FAA and the agency's highest-ranking security manager, wrote to Lawless asking him to "reconsider his policy" of conducting background checks. Canavan wrote that "concern" over the Massport checks had been raised by the airlines during an April 19 meeting of the Air Transport Association and the Regional Airline Association. "I am asking your help in the resolution of this situation, and ask that you accept certification from U.S. air carriers that the required criminal history records check has been completed for their employees."[29]

On May 30, 2001, Canavan wrote to the Federal Security Managers of the New England region of the FAA:[30]

> The safety and security of the flying public will depend upon the FAA and industry maintaining a candid, respectful, and mutually responsive relationship. To be effective in this relationship, we need to be flexible.

Canavan went on to say:

While I expect regulated parties to comply with regulatory requirements, there will be times when we find areas of noncompliance. When we do, I want to fully consider the actions the party has taken to fix the problem.

In what can only be described as an abrogation of the agency's authority over the airlines, the letter detailed the FAA's new philosophy when it came to working with the airlines on matters of security:

I want to work with industry to develop action plans to permanently correct problems that have resulted in violations. To encourage industry to join us in this effort I do not expect us to impose a civil penalty against a regulated party for certain aggravated violations.

The letter concluded by affirming the idea of a partnership between the FAA and the airlines:

I want to continue to give our partners a realistic opportunity to comply with the regulations and to work with us.

On July 11, as a result of the WFXT television report two months earlier, Safety Director Lawless and Massachusetts State Police Major John Kelly announced at a public safety staff meeting that they were ready to begin undercover testing of security checkpoints. Up until that point, however, the only testing on security checkpoints at Logan had been done by the FAA. But under its testing program, the FAA kept records between itself and the airlines, and did not share them with Massport.[31]

A week later, at a meeting of the Logan Airlines Manager's Council (LAMCO), Lawless presented his plan. The feedback from the airlines and the FAA to this proposal was swift and powerful. The immediate response from the airlines and Logan Airport's FAA Federal Security Manager (FSM), Steve Luongo, was to thwart Lawless's idea. The airlines were worried the test results would be shared with the FAA or others.[32] The plan was shelved and nothing was ever done.

Even more revealing, a security consortium—one of the recommendations of the Gore Commission—was never established by Massport. The consortium, which was to include representatives from the airport, airlines, law enforcement, FAA, Massport, and others, was supposed to discuss openly security issues like the one proposed by Lawless. However, at Logan, the airline manager's council was used in its place. Therefore, instead of having any real debate or discussion on security matters affecting the airport, everything was deferred to the airlines and their final judgment.

In an e-mail dated August 16, 2001, from Brian Sullivan to FAA Security Chief Michael Canavan, the retired FAA agent elaborated again upon the continuing situation at Logan and the façade of aviation security that existed there.[33] To his credit, Canavan responded to Sullivan's e-mail on August 22 and admitted security at Logan wasn't up to standards, but that he was taking action to get things fixed.[34] Twenty days later, at 7:59 A.M., American flight 11 departed Logan for Los Angeles from gate 26 in terminal B with ninety-two people on board. Fifteen minutes after that, United flight 175, also bound for L.A., departed gate 19 in terminal C with sixty-five people on board. Less than three hours later, the World Trade Center in New York would be a smoldering ruin and nearly three thousand innocent people would be dead.

# CHAPTER 3

# THE GREAT BAILOUT

"Crime doesn't pay . . . as well as politics . . ."

—Alfred E. Neuman

Just before 8:30 A.M. on Tuesday, September 11, 2001, air traffic controllers knew that terror was in the air. They realized that two planes departing Boston's Logan had been hijacked and had reversed their westbound courses in favor of a jagged flight path toward New York City. Between 8:40 and 8:43 A.M., FAA officials made two calls to the North American Aerospace Defense Command. Within minutes, two F-15 fighter planes took off from Otis Air National Guard Base in Falmouth, Massachusetts, to try to limit, if not prevent, casualties. But it was too late.

Minutes later, federal officials ordered a halt to all air traffic flying in and out of New York. At the same time, air traffic controllers picked up on their radar a third potential flying bomb, American Airlines flight 77, departing from Washington's Dulles International Airport. Again the Defense Department was called. Three F-15s immediately took off from Langley Air Force Base, Virginia.

By 9:25 A.M., the unprecedented action was taken to order all aircraft out of the sky. Domestic flights were ordered to land immediately at the nearest airport. In-bound international flights were sent to Canada. Only two planes ignored the order. One, flight 77, crashed into the Pentagon at 9:43. The other, United Airlines flight 93, crashed near the town of Shanksville in rural Somerset County, Pennsylvania, twenty-three minutes later, at 10:06 A.M.

Within two hours of the order being issued, thousands of commercial flights had been landed and the skies over America were quieter than anyone alive could ever remember. For the next forty-eight hours, nothing flew. Everything was grounded. Not until the afternoon of Thursday, September 14, air cargo planes began to move once again. On Friday, passenger flights began to take off and the system started to return to some semblance of normalcy. By Saturday, 70 percent of aviation service was up and running across the country.

## THE INDUSTRY GETS TO WORK

Clearly, the hijackings and the death and destruction they wrought dramatically jolted the air travel industry. However, nearly as shocking as the tragic events of 9/11 were the Bush administration's and Congress's almost unconditional and unquestioning support of the airlines following the terrorist attacks. Hours after the World Trade Center towers collapsed, the airline industry's political machine kicked into full gear, laying the foundation for a multibillion-dollar scheme to bail out the industry. Twenty-seven in-house lobbyists along with another group of lobbyists working for forty-two Washington firms and the CEOs of several major carriers went to work lining up congressional support for a massive cash infusion of taxpayer money into the industry. "It was masterful," said Sen. Peter Fitzgerald, an Illinois Republican, the lone dissenter in the Senate to federal assistance to the airlines. "The

The FAA-ordered shutdown of the nation's entire air transport system after the September 11 attacks was an unprecedented event in aviation history. Every airport in the country was silenced.

airline industry made a full-court press to convince Congress that giving them billions in taxpayer cash was the only way to save the Republic."[1]

Linda Daschle; Haley Barbour, former chairman of the Republican National Committee; and Rebecca Cox, a former Reagan administration official and the wife of U.S. Representative Christopher Cox, were part of an army deployed to work back halls and offices to drum up support for the plan on Capitol Hill. Leading the charge were several airline CEOs, many of whom were big contributors to the Bush campaign in 2000. Among them were Donald Carty, CEO of American Airlines, and Gordon Bethune, chief executive of Continental Airlines, both based in Texas and who have known the Bush family for years. "It was the most high-level surgical strike that I have ever seen," said Jeff Munk, a partner at the Washington law firm of Hogan and Hartson and a lobbyist for General Electric, which makes jet engines and leases aircraft. "And the people who made it happen were the CEOs."[2]

In addition to the lobbyists and CEOs, at private meetings held on Capitol Hill—while fires still raged at the Pentagon and the World Trade Center—several aviation experts were consulted about what should be done. Daryl Jenkins, director of the Aviation Institute at George Washington University, was one such expert. Jenkins gave congressional leaders his stamp of approval on the same bailout that was being lobbied for by the industry. The massive cash infusion would be a shot in the arm for the reeling industry, he reasoned, and would send a message to terrorists that America would not allow them to knock out such a vital industry.[3]

Not surprisingly, in a *USA Today* article a few months later, Jenkins admitted he had been a well-paid consultant for almost every airline and never charged more than the "low six figures" for an annual contract.[4] In the days after September 11, the fleet of experts and consultants on the payroll of the airlines were sought out by many in Congress to substantiate the amount and method of an industry bailout. A senior American Airlines official, who was unnamed, said, "There's a long-standing practice in Washington of supporting people who support you. American has a bunch of consultants charged with going out and building support for issues we support."[5] To Mr. Jenkins's credit, he did not attempt to hide his affiliation with the industry, like many in his profession. When asked about his consulting contracts, he stated, "I'm the only one who won't lie to you."[6]

To further strengthen their case, board members of the six major airlines made personal phone calls to leading members of Congress and the Bush administration. Kirbyjon Caldwell, a Continental director, reportedly phoned three senators, saying the bailout was needed to transform "a moment of fear to a moment of faith." An American Airlines director, John Bachmann, purportedly called Missouri Congressmen Dick Gephardt and Roy Blount to say the industry's losses were nothing less than "breathtaking" and required immediate action.[7]

Eight days after the attacks, with the groundwork laid in place, the CEOs of Delta Airlines, Alaska Airlines, America West Airlines, Federal Express, and Northwest Airlines, along with the CFO for American Airlines were on Capitol Hill in front of the House Committee on Transportation and Infrastructure, seeking immediate financial support from the government. Delta chief Leo Mullin, who served as the spokesman for the group, outlined the needs of the industry. For most Americans, some degree of taxpayer assistance to the airlines was reasonable, especially since the government-ordered shutdown of all air traffic had cost the industry hundreds of millions of dollars. The only question seemed to be: how much assistance? According to the industry's own analysis and testimony before Congress, the shutdown cost $340 million a day in lost revenue. That adds up to $1.36 billion (assuming a four-day as opposed to a three-day shutdown). This amount seemed legitimate to many. Nevertheless, the airlines eventually got the government to give them billions and billions more over the next months.

The major carriers asked Congress for "an immediate $5 billion cash allocation to address the immediate and devastating impact of September 11 on our industry." In addition, the CEOs asked the government to provide them with access to billions more in loan guarantees.[8] But there was more. The CEOs requested that Congress "pass legislation preserving any existing rights of proper parties to bring claims against the airlines for the experiences and existing deaths of the airlines' passengers." However, such legislation would also stipulate, based on the fact that this was an act of war, "that the airlines would not be liable for the damage to persons and property on the ground." In other words, the airlines would be freed from any legal liability for those who died at the Pentagon, the World Trade Center, or Shanksville. In addition, the airlines proposed that Congress expand the war risk insurance program to include domestic operations and assist wherever possible in providing airlines with insurance coverage.[9]

The requests continued. The industry asked Congress to have the federal government take over all the responsibilities and costs associated with aviation security. The airlines asked the government to "provide financial support for all mandated safety requirements, including reinforcement of cockpit doors and enhancement of screening devices," as well as "take over all security screening functions" and the requisite costs associated with it.

To reassure the taxpayers they wouldn't merely be writing a blank check to the airlines, the industry promised to Congress that they "would fully document each and every claim received from both the cash infusion and the credit facility . . . under the administration of the Department of Transportation."[10] This was the same Department of Transportation that was charged with overseeing the industry for the past several decades. And, attempting to alleviate any remaining concerns, the airline CEOs insisted that their request was "not a bailout, but rather a package designed solely to recover the damages associated with the heinous acts of September 11 . . . and offer the public service it is [their] duty to provide."[11]

# THE AIR TRANSPORTATION SAFETY AND STABILIZATION ACT

A mere eleven days after the attacks, President George W. Bush signed into law the Air Transportation Safety and System Stabilization Act.[12] In the House the vote for the bailout was an overwhelming 356 to 54. In the Senate, the vote went 96 in favor of the bailout and 1—Peter Fitzgerald—against. Bluntly put, the airlines got all they wanted and even more.

Title I of the law earmarked $15 billion to the industry: $5 billion in grants (or, in other words, free money) and $10 billion in secured loans. Other add-ons followed. Title II stated that any increases in insurance premiums charged to the airlines would be reimbursed by the federal government. Title IV dealt with the issue of victim compensation. Spelled out was the manner in which the federal government insured the airlines' inculpability. It offered the 9/11 victims' families $1.6 million each in taxpayer money if they signed a waiver forgoing their right to sue. In Title V, the law guaranteed that the federal government would now absorb the responsibility *and* the cost of aviation security across the United States forever. This freed the airlines from an estimated $1.2 billion in annual security costs and passed the buck to the taxpayers.

Senator Fitzgerald argued that the bailout plan was unfair to workers and unfair to taxpayers. He recognized a strong case existed for compensating the airlines for the temporary government-ordered shutdown of air travel, but, "Congress went way beyond this mandate in favor of the airlines, and eventually did write a blank check to the airlines."[13]

Commenting on the airlines' efforts, Representative George Miller, a California Democrat, summed it up when he said, "The big dog got the bone. After September 11, the mood was one of shared sacrifice. People had lost their jobs and their lives. And the first thing that happened was the airline industry came in while everyone else is waiting to see if they can make their mortgage payments."[14]

# THE FALLOUT FROM THE BAILOUT

After the bailout was secured, the industry did pretty much what it wanted to with no strings attached. The carriers sucked up the $5 billion in cash with no problem. At the same time, almost one hundred thousand employees were fired, and air transport service was cut off for millions of Americans living in small communities. Meanwhile, costly business ventures continued to be explored and funded by the carriers.

One element that was never brought up during the debate was the fact that the airlines weren't doing very well financially on September 10, 2001. After recovering from a downturn in the early 1990s, caused in part by the Gulf War and a recession, the airline industry enjoyed its most prosperous period in history. Record profits and an exponential rise in the number of passengers traveling every year gave the airlines the very real impression that high growth could always be assumed. Throughout the mid- to late '90s, it was not uncommon for a last-minute business traveler to pay $2,000 to fly from Los Angeles to San Francisco or $1,800 to go from Cleveland to Boston. Business was good all across America and the airlines were cashing in.

During 1998 and 1999, the major carriers, believing they were invincible, overextended themselves, buying too many planes and overcharging their best customers—business travelers. As the dot.com bubble burst in early 2000 and the economy slowed, business travelers—who accounted for as much as 80 percent of airlines' profits—cut back on travel. Companies dramatically reduced the number of times they sent their employees out to do business. Corporate travel departments were now ordered to shop for the lowest fare and book trips far in advance for lower prices. The significant drop in this customer demographic, coupled with higher fuel prices throughout the first half of 2001, threatened airline profitability and pushed some companies to the verge of bankruptcy well before the September 11 attacks.

Robert Crandall, former CEO of American, commented on the problems of the airlines prior to the attacks when he observed, "I'm not sure 9/11 by itself had any particularly profound impact [on the industry]. But it exacerbated the problems they had before 9/11."[15] Duane Woerth, president of the Air Line Pilots Association, was among many who saw the economics of air travel fundamentally changing before 9/11. "When the stock market popped, the airlines held onto this pricing model where they tried to make all their money off 20 percent of the travelers."[16]

A September 19, 2001, editorial in the *Wall Street Journal* blasted the idea of the bailout, stating: "Other industries are now suffering through the same devastating aftermath of the terrorist attack. Insurance companies are facing costs that could total $20 to $30 billion. After airlines get their money, what's to stop politicians from tapping taxpayers to bail out every other industry?"

The industry did nothing to obscure the fact that despite the multibillion-dollar bailout, tens of thousands of airline employees would be fired. Nearly every major carrier fired at least 20 percent of its staff, with United Airlines and American Airlines both cutting twenty thousand jobs. US Airways fired the biggest percentage of its workforce, 23 percent, and laid off eleven thousand workers. Delta and Continental fired thirteen thousand and twelve thousand employees respectively after receiving the bailout funds.[17]

A few days after the taxpayers' money started flowing from the U.S. Treasury, the parent company of United Airlines made a down payment on thirty brand-new luxury business jets. The purchase was part of a new strategy that United had embarked on to sell shares of aircrafts to corporations, celebrities, and other wealthy individuals. Representative Peter DeFazio, an Oregon Democrat, remarked on the purchase, "It's outrageous. On one hand they say they need an immediate cash infusion from the government, no strings attached, and on the other they are wiring money to France."[18]

Notwithstanding the fact that Section 105 of the new law instructed the secretary of the DOT "to ensure that all communities that had scheduled air service before September 11, 2001, continue to receive adequate air transportation," service was immediately cut to dozens of cities around the country by the airlines. Several members of the House and Senate who days before had supported the airline bailout found themselves at loggerheads with the same industry that was now cutting air service to their constituents.

By the end of October 2001, twenty-five Congressional members petitioned the Department of Transportation to step in to preserve the now eliminated air routes that were supposedly protected by the same legislation they had passed five weeks earlier. Senator Blanche Lincoln, a Democrat from Arkansas, complained that United had eliminated its service to Little Rock, leaving the airport there with no nonstop service to Chicago's O'Hare International. "What we wanted was to be able to get the airlines back on their feet," Lincoln said of the bailout. "To pull out completely in certain markets is not in the spirit in which we embarked on that legislation."[19]

Rep. Bob Goodlatte, a Republican from Virginia, mirrored Lincoln's frustration when United cut service to Roanoke, Lynchburg, and Weyers Cave, Virginia. "My constituents are paying taxes like everyone else. They shouldn't be disproportionately hurt in the routes that are cut."[20]

Clearly, the actions taken by the airlines immediately after they secured the assistance of the U.S. taxpayers were not in agreement with what President Bush publicly stated when he authorized the bailout eleven days after more than three thousand people had been killed. The president assured all Americans that the legislation would provide urgently needed tools to assure the safety and immediate stability of our nation's commercial airline system. The terrorists who attacked our country on September 11 would not shut down our vital businesses or thwart our way of life.

Beyond the billions transferred from the pockets of taxpayers to the coffers of the airlines as a result of the bailout, the industry received billions more in tax refunds through a loophole in an economic stimulus bill signed by the president in March 2002. Under a previous law, airlines could use only losses from one year to offset tax obligations in the previous two years. However, under the new law, businesses, including the airlines, were able to extend their losses over a five-year period. In this case, it included the years 1996–2000—the industry's most profitable period ever.[21] Estimates placed the refunds for some of the major carriers at about $464 million for United and around $200 million each for US Airways, American, and Delta.[22]

## THE SECURITY BAILOUT

At the same time the industry and its fellow travelers were hard at work convincing the administration and Congress about the need for government assistance, many were also trying to convince the federal government to take over all the responsibilities and costs associated with aviation security. In the short term, along with the bailout money, Congress authorized the president to spend immediately $3 billion on aviation security after 9/11. Even though some aspects of security—passenger and baggage screening in particular—were still under the control of the airlines, the taxpayer was asked to pay for any additional costs related to beefing up the system. Moreover, there was little if any debate as to whether the federal government would step in and take over all aspects of aviation security.

On September 16, 2001, Secretary of Transportation Norman Mineta announced the creation of two Rapid Response teams to deliver detailed recommendations for improving security within the national aviation system. The teams were designed to augment the work of senior DOT and FAA experts with eight national leaders in aviation and security protection. As the groups were formed, Secretary Mineta announced, "These are complex issues, but we have a strong base on which to build. We can and will build on existing analysis as the Department of Transportation prepares to act on specific recommendations. I'm confident that each of these distinguished Rapid Response teams will help us do just that."[23]

Operating under the Federal Advisory Committee Act that requires membership of an advisory committee be fairly balanced in terms of the points of view represented, the Rapid Response teams were tipped in the favor of the airlines. Even a passing glance at the members reveals the airline industry would influence the teams' recommendations. More important, whatever conclusions were formed by the Rapid Response teams were to serve as the foundation for the national debate on aviation security in the following weeks. And, as we'll explore later, the post 9/11 version of aviation security came to be eerily similar to the system that existed on September 11, 2001. That is, with the airlines and market forces more than any other groups determining what could and couldn't be done in the area of aviation security.

The teams were formed into two groups: aircraft security and airport security. The members of the aircraft security team included Robert W. Baker, vice chairman of American Airlines; Robert A. Davis, former vice president of engineering and technology for Boeing; Richard H. Anderson, chief executive officer for Northwest Airlines; and, Duane Woerth, president of the Air Line Pilots Association. The airport security team consisted of Herb Kelleher, CEO of Southwest Airlines; Charles Barclay, president of the American Association of Airport Executives; Patricia Friend, president of the Association of Flight Attendants; and, Ray Kelly, former New York City Police Commissioner.

In all, the eight people chosen by the federal government to lead the way on new aviation security policy included three commercial airline executives, two presidents of airline unions, one representative of a trade association of airport managers, and a retired executive from Boeing. Only one member, Ray Kelly, had a law enforcement background. None had any aviation security experience.[24]

Gail Dunham, president of the National Air Disaster Alliance Foundation, a public advocacy group, concurred. "To give the airlines more money to recover from their financial problems and to have the airlines and government schmooze to work out the security problems is not the answer. We can't have the industry governing itself."[25]

In what would come to be commonplace in the upcoming debate about aviation security in Washington, the Department of Transportation reinforced the notion of the airlines' leading the way in establishing new policy. Lenny Alcivar, a DOT spokesperson, said the heavy emphasis on airline industry representatives was appropriate because of their familiarity with aviation practices and because their industry's future depends on convincing passengers that it is safe to fly again. "The nature of our aviation industry is undergoing fundamental change," Alcivar said. "It would be intellectually dishonest not to have their [airlines'] input when we work through this new paradigm for aviation."[26] When it came to aviation security immediately after the 9/11 attacks, it seemed, at least in the short term, nothing had really changed. The industry was still the dominant player.

# CHAPTER 4

# THE AVIATION SECURITY RESPONSE TO 9/11

"You can't buy security."

—Anonymous

**B**y every discernible measure, the aviation security system in place on September 11, 2001, failed miserably. Through low-tech but effective tactics, coupled with a strong dedication to strategic planning, the terrorists successfully leveraged several of the glaring weaknesses of the system to their favor. Insecure cockpit doors, lax passenger screening standards, flawed policy requiring flight attendants to carry cockpit keys, and neglecting to deal with disruptive passengers were systemic weaknesses exploited by the hijackers to meet their ends. The stark reality of the breakdown of the system began to compel everyone in aviation security to question what the future would hold.

From nearly the same moment as the World Trade Center towers collapsed, the national concern with preventing another suicide hijacking understandably verged on the point of frantic obsession. Cockpit doors were reinforced. National guardsmen were dispatched to airports around the country. Military jets patrolled the skies, prepared to shoot down any hijacked aircraft. Suspicious behavior on the ground or in a plane most often resulted in a terminal being evacuated or a plane being escorted by a fighter jet at its side.

Obviously, the terrorist attacks of 9/11 created an immediate crisis of confidence in the civil aviation system. The fallout was evident everywhere. Passengers canceled vacation plans. Corporations put a halt to their employees' travel schedules. The number of empty seats on flights skyrocketed. At hotels, resorts, and rental car counters across the country, employees often outnumbered guests. In short, commercial aviation was experiencing the biggest shock in its history and it was affecting other industries. Something needed to be done and done immediately.

The Travel Industry Association spent a small fortune on patriotic advertisements, blazing images across American television sets, radio stations, and billboards. These ads implied that Americans had a responsibility as good citizens to travel, spend their money, and prove that the American way of life was stronger than the actions of global terrorists. In response to the call of duty, many Americans found themselves asking: "How about the duty of the airline industry and the federal government to fix their problems?"

At the FAA, a predictable yet controversial shake-up began to occur. Michael Canavan, head of security, quit in protest less than a month after the attacks. By all accounts, Canavan—who was only in the job position for about nine months—possessed splendid credentials for the job, along with a tough, serious mind. He spent thirty-four years in the U.S. Army, enlisting during Vietnam and serving much of his time with Special Forces. He seemed to bring to the FAA that special quality of urgency and concentration that comes from being shot at with live ammunition.[1] For those who knew the retired lieutenant general, the resignation came totally unexpectedly. The announcement was even more stunning since, in an e-mail message to all FAA Civil Aviation Security employees sent September 22, 2001, two weeks before he resigned, Canavan said he was committed to staying on:

> Prior to last week's events there were rumors that I would be moving on to another position in Washington. I want you to know that I have no plans to leave and that I am fully committed to instilling the public's confidence back in our Civil Aviation System. . . . Now is the time to do the right things in terms of security which is after all, our "Sense of Purpose."[2]

According to several FAA insiders, they believed Canavan was forced out of the job. This theory flew in the face of what a DOT press release described as "a mutual agreement to move on" between Mr. Canavan and FAA Administrator Jane Garvey.[3] An employee at FAA headquarters said Canavan, who held the position for less than ten months, was pushed out because of his desire to reform the FAA's security functions. "The general feeling among the troops is that Canavan was the one hope we had to reform the agency. Even before the attacks, he was starting to change how we did business."[4]

Others believed the highest ranking aviation security official in the United States left his job in protest. In the days immediately after the terrorist attacks, nine Cabinet members announced they would take commercial flights to show the nation that flying was safe, trying to re-instill some degree of confidence in the system. At the request of his superiors, Canavan was ordered to reassign air marshals from their normally scheduled flights to those that were carrying the Cabinet members. Canavan argued that the flights air marshals were currently assigned to presented more of a risk of hijacking than those flights that would be taken by the government officials. If overruled, Canavan had told some people at the FAA that he would resign.[5]

Whatever the ultimate reason for Canavan's leaving, the departure of the FAA's head of aviation security in such a manner helped to build the case that the agency simply was no longer capable of handling the responsibility. Conventional wisdom began to hold that the FAA was too bogged down in internal strife and too close to the airline industry to implement real security changes. Many in Congress who had been historically fervent supporters of the present security system were beginning to question whether aviation security, as it had evolved, would be better left outside the influences of market forces. It seemed there was finally a real recognition of the culture of compromise that had dominated the FAA for decades. Sen. Max Cleland, a Georgia Democrat and member of the Senate Commerce, Science, and Transportation Committee, began to reflect the mood of many on Capitol Hill after the attacks when he said, "What happened is we dumbed down the security system, because an airline is going to want to cut costs, specifically when we have a downturn in the economy and they are fighting for their lives."[6]

Further bringing the issue to a head was the always present but too-often-disregarded element of suicidal terrorists exploiting the system. Suicidal attacks on commercial aviation prior to 9/11 were nothing new. Unfortunately, however, many key decision makers in the U.S. had failed to ever take into serious account this threat before the attacks. And, although the notion of an individual killing himself in the pursuit of inflicting greater damage on his enemy is as old as conflict itself, the magnitude of the 9/11 attacks compelled leaders to consider this possibility in a new way. The paradigm of aviation security had changed and a new way of keeping aviation safe was needed.

It was now clear to even the most casual observer that hijackings could no longer be treated as mere political actions with flight crews and passengers submitting themselves to orders from terrorists. Airports, some of the busiest and most populated places in our society, now had to be considered prime targets for a suicide bomber looking to detonate a weapon of mass destruction and kill thousands in a terminal or concourse. And, aircraft of all sizes needed to be better secured so that they could not serve as a delivery system for that death and destruction.

To force the issue of the FAA relinquishing control of security, several congressional leaders began to cite the agency's long-practiced system of levying fines on carriers for security violations—rather than seeking harsher corrective actions for airlines—as evidence of the agency's compromise with market forces. Over time, the system had developed to the point that fines would be negotiated down at special administrative hearings. Moreover, the carriers considered the final amounts to be simply a cost of doing business rather than an impetus to improve security. In 1999, the last full year of available records, Delta was cited for 729 security violations; United, 661; and American, 555. In the two-year period 1997–98, those three airlines were cited for a total of 3,552 violations. Michael Pangia, former chief counsel at the FAA, observed that "it's a common practice" for the airlines and the FAA to negotiate fines down to as low as ten cents on the dollar. "It's obvious the airlines don't want these breaches, but it is a whole lot easier to pay the fines. And the FAA thought they were doing their job, because they were fining people. But when they keep levying the same fines year after year after year, they ought to wake up and say there is something wrong with this system."[7]

The end result of the criticisms against the FAA's inability to oversee the aviation security system was the movement toward the government taking over complete responsibility of the function. The urgency of this undertaking was critical. Senator Cleland said further, "We've got to move fast on this, because the airlines are bleeding. Unless they get 65 percent capacity in that cabin they don't make any money. So, security is number one in a series of confidence building measures that will bring people back to fly."[8]

The industry worked hard pressuring Congress for a total and complete takeover of the aviation security system. Carol Hallett, president of the Air Transport Association declared, "Today, airport security is no longer a passenger issue. It is an issue of national security. Our planes were used as missiles of mass destruction. And, unless the national security of America is maintained by the government and not just airlines and their passengers, the terrorists will win!"[9]

In addition, a consensus beyond the air lines was building for a federal takeover. In an October 30, 2001, letter to congressional leaders urging the federalization of the aviation security system, several noted citizens' groups as well as airline employee unions and passenger associations encouraged Congress to move quickly.

> It is high time to recognize that the private sector operations of the nation's aviation security system under government regulation over the past 30 years have failed and must be replaced with a federal government operated system.[10]

The American public wanted action as well. A Gallup poll conducted just days before the attacks asked Americans whether the government was trying to do too many things that should be left to individuals and businesses, or whether it should do more to solve the country's problems. Fifty-five percent thought the government was doing too much, compared with 36 percent who thought it should do more. When the same poll was repeated a few weeks after the 9/11 attacks, the results flipped; 41 percent thought the government was doing too much, while 51 percent believed it should do more to solve the country's problems.[11]

Specific to aviation security, in a *Newsweek* survey just after the attacks, when asked what would be "very effective" in preventing similar terrorist attacks, the public rated "more security at airports" (76 percent) and in-flight precautions like air marshals and locked cockpit doors (75 percent) ahead of military strikes (49 percent) and killing suspected terrorist leaders (44 percent).[12]

General agreement across the country was emerging that the government's assumption of a stronger role in aviation security would be a crucial step that would go far in resolving public concerns over the safety of the system. The federalization of the aviation security system seemed a foregone conclusion. The only real debate seemed to be about how that system would look under full government control.

## WHERE TO PUT AVIATION SECURITY WITHIN THE FEDERAL GOVERNMENT?

At the outset of the aviation security deliberations, Congress appeared not to be debating whether the government would take over the entire system or not. Like Congress, the Bush administration favored moving security duties out of the FAA and into a new agency in Transportation that would handle security for all modes of transportation. The FAA supported the move, even though it knew it would lose some employees to the TSA, according to administrator Jane Garvey. "I would not characterize [our position] as reluctance at all," she says. "We were strongly advocating for an agency that had a single focus of security." Instead, the issues of highest priority were: which government department would be charged with the aviation security function; and, what would be the ultimate status of airport security screeners. Both issues served as focal points for the deliberations that Congress embarked upon in the eight weeks following the terrorist attacks.

The airlines, not surprisingly, put their considerable weight behind keeping the Department of Transportation in control of aviation security. For years, the airlines had, in many ways, shaped the decisions taken by DOT and FAA in their favor. Intensive lobbying and direct campaign contributions to key Congressional members, including most who sat on the House and Senate Transportation Committees, may have helped put DOT firmly in the corner of the carriers.

To substantiate the idea that DOT should be in charge of any new security agency, the airlines and their allies argued that placing the function outside of DOT would delay the implementation of any pending legislation. The United States has the largest civil aviation system in the world, exponentially bigger than any other country. Forty percent of all worldwide passenger air traffic occurs within the United States. The system is breathtakingly large: nineteen thousand airports; nearly 650 million passengers flying each year; more than 1 billion passenger bags handled each year; and 450 million tons of freight transported annually. Every day there are almost thirty thousand commercial flights that transport about 2 million passengers. In 2002, approximately seven thousand air traffic controllers at 475 commercial airports supervised over 68.5 million takeoffs and landings. The industry claimed that a failure to keep aviation security within the purview of DOT would weaken the benefit of years of expertise.

The basis for reasons against the DOT overseeing a new federal aviation security agency stemmed from fears that market forces would ultimately dictate policy and compromise public safety as they had in the past. Airlines and airports are in the business of providing public transportation, the argument went. Further, the DOT is not a national security or primary law enforcement agency. Therefore, trying to reinforce the present system by adding another level of federal supervision and regulation to DOT was likely to fail.

As for the ultimate status of airport screeners, several options were explored on Capitol Hill. They ranged from turning the approximately thirty thousand checkpoint employees into full federal employees under the control of the FAA; to having the screeners placed under the domain of a new federal agency charged with aviation security; or, to be placed into an existing law enforcement agency of the federal government.

The first option, of FAA oversight of the screeners as federal employees, was briefly discussed and then later dismissed as congressional members increasingly recognized that the FAA's failure to regulate the airline industry was in large part responsible for the failures of 9/11. John Mica, a Florida republican and chairman of the powerful House Transportation and Aviation Subcommittee, spoke for many when he said, "The FAA has been directed by Congress twice—in 1996 and 2000—to come up with standards and certification of screeners. And still to this day it doesn't have it in place. Why would I turn over 27,000 employees to an agency that did not have in place any rules to prohibit box cutters?"[13]

Consequently, the question of who would be in charge of the airport screeners paralleled the question that asked which federal agency would be charged with the aviation security function. Would it be a brand new agency created within the DOT with thirty thousand or so new employees? Or, would the responsibility of aviation security and all the personnel and funds associated with it be transferred from DOT to another already-existing federal agency?

Given what we know about the relationship between the airline industry and its supporters on Capitol Hill, the answer came as no surprise whatsoever. A new federal agency, under the control and jurisdiction of the DOT, was created by Congress to assume all civil aviation security functions and responsibilities that had been previously performed by the FAA. With the DOT still in charge, the airlines and their friends in Congress would be still be able to influence any decisions made by the new agency in charge of aviation security.

## THE AVIATION AND TRANSPORTATION SECURITY ACT

The legislation that took away the FAA's aviation security role and gave it to the newly formed Transportation Security Administration (TSA) under the DOT was signed into law by President George W. Bush on November 19, 2001. In his remarks immediately after signing the Aviation and Transportation Security Act (ATSA), the president sounded supremely confident in government's ability to build confidence back into the commercial aviation system:

> For the first time, aviation security will become a direct federal responsibility. . . . Security comes first. The federal government will set high standards, and we will enforce them. A proud industry has been hit hard. But this nation has seen the dedication and spirit of our pilots and flight crews, and the hundreds of

thousands of hard-working people who keep America flying. We know they will endure. I'm confident this industry will grow and prosper.[14]

The new legislation made the TSA responsible for the day-to-day security screening operations for passenger air transportation and interstate air transportation. That responsibility included hiring, training, testing, and deploying or arranging for federal security screeners, federal security personnel, federal law enforcement officers, and federal security managers at all U.S. airports. The TSA was also mandated to research, develop, and deploy security equipment and programs at U.S. airports, coordinate transportation security intelligence information, coordinate transportation security efforts with federal and state agencies, and deal with threats to transportation.[15]

The legislation was quite bold in establishing deadlines for several activities that Congress believed would strengthen aviation security for the long-term. Nevertheless, as we'll see later, the details spelled out within each of the requirements were not as courageous as they first appeared. Among the deadlines were:

| Congressional Activity | Deadline |
| --- | --- |
| Deploy federal screeners and related personnel at all U.S. airports. | November 19, 2002 |
| Establish a pilot program for screening by private entities. | November 19, 2002 |
| Ensure sufficient Explosive Detection Systems (EDS) to screen all checked baggage at all U.S. airports. | December 31, 2002 |

Under the new legislation, all functions related to aviation security previously under the control of the FAA were to be transferred to the TSA. Personnel, property, records, unexpended fund balances, and all related authority from the FAA also were transferred to the TSA. Existing FAA orders, rules, regulations, grants, and proceedings were to remain in effect until modified, terminated, superseded, set aside, or revoked.

Congress and the president also encouraged the TSA to explore optional enhanced security measures, including:

- ✈ Providing for 911 emergency call capability on passenger aircraft
- ✈ Generating a uniform ID system for state and local law enforcement officers carrying weapons on aircraft or in secure areas
- ✈ Issuing requirements for a trusted traveler program
- ✈ Using technology for secure plane-to-ground threat communication
- ✈ Developing photo and biometric imprints on all pilot licenses
- ✈ Assessing voice stress biometric technology for screening potential threats
- ✈ Implementing instant air-to-ground communications

To offset the costs of providing civil aviation security services, the TSA was to impose a uniform fee on passenger enplanements beginning February 1, 2002. A corresponding fee on both U.S. and foreign air carriers was to be assessed based on their calendar year 2000 costs for screening passengers and property. Briefly stated, in the mere nine weeks after the 9/11 attacks, aviation security policy in the United States had undergone its most comprehensive and radical transformation in history, at least on paper. The real test would come when it was time to put the new system in place.

# CHAPTER 5

# THE BUSINESS OF AVIATION AND THE NEW SECURITY REGIMEN

"Deregulation will be the greatest thing to happen to the airlines since the jet engine."

—Richard Ferris, CEO, United Airlines, 1976

Aviation is one of our nation's and the world's most important businesses. The growth of the industry over the past decades has made it one of the engines for the expansion of the United States and, in fact, the global economy. The aviation industry has driven a substantial part of the economic and social integration that has brought much of the world closer together and helped make the United States the dominant player on the global stage. By moving hundreds of millions of passengers and billions of tons of cargo each year, the industry has changed the way of life for most human beings on this planet. Distance is now often measured in hours rather than weeks or months. New York to Hong Kong takes thirteen hours by air—thirty-five days by sea. Manufactured goods produced in Chicago can be transported to distributors in Ouagadougou, Burkina Faso, within forty-eight hours. UPS and

Federal Express can deliver an envelope from Cleveland to Tashkent, Uzbekistan, in seventy-two hours. The aviation industry has changed forever the way many human beings look at the world around them.

Nevertheless, the industry itself is more than merely the transportation of goods and people. It is a massive enterprise that directly employs approximately 4 million individuals worldwide, about half of them in the United States. In addition, millions of others are employed in businesses and industries that support, service, or are directly affected by the aviation industry. Moreover, the number of customers and stakeholders of the industry is in the billions. They come from every sector of the world's economy and from every segment of the world's population.[1] (See table 3, below.)

Yet, despite its wide scope and impact, the economic supports of the aviation industry are inherently fragile, even in the best of times. Historically, the industry has always had to walk a very fine line between profits and losses. From 1997 to 2001, when the industry in the United States enjoyed record profits in three out of five years, airlines were still not able to generate a return on capital that was higher than the average of the companies that make up the Standard and Poor's 500 stock index.[2]

In fact, according to Kevin Murphy, the top aviation analyst at Morgan Stanley and one of the most respected experts on the subject, the airline industry has created little wealth and has not earned a return exceeding its cost of capital for most of the years since the industry was deregulated in 1978. Despite the great bailout of the industry by the federal government following the 9/11 attacks, the major U.S. carriers managed to lose $7.7 billion. In the first quarter of 2002, the losses continued to grow to another $2.4 billion. By mid-2002, the industry was carrying an on-balance-sheet debt of nearly $110 billion, with debt-to-capital ratios more than double those of other industries.[3] Murphy concludes: "The business model of the existing companies is just flat-out broken."[4]

# Table 3. Key Stakeholders of the Aviation Industry

| Manufacturers | Carriers | Directly Served |
|---|---|---|
| Airframes/Engines | Major airlines | Passengers |
| Mechanical systems | Regional airlines | Rental cars/Parking |
| Computers/Electronics | Charter airlines | Other ground transport |
| Information systems | Special services | Hotels/Restaurants |
| Software | Air cargo carriers | Tourism/Attractions |
| Materials/Chemicals | General aviation | Retail |
| | | Travel agents |
| | | Cruise lines |
| | | Conventions |
| Governments | **Air** | Employees |
| Aviation authorities | | Manufacturers |
| Legislative bodies | **Transport** | Airlines |
| Regulatory agencies | | Airports |
| Customs | **Industry** | Cargo |
| Air traffic control | | Aviation services |
| | | Bureaucrats |
| **Aviation Services** | **Airports** | **Cargo** |
| Insurance | Major airports | Freight forwarders |
| Leasing/Financing | General aviation airports | Warehousing |
| Distributors | Training centers | Consolidation |
| Telecommunications | Terminal maintenance | Mail |
| Maintenance | Catering/Inflight services | Transport |
| Fuel and oil | Air traffic control | |
| Training | | |
| Universities | | |

On October 9, 2002, the stock price of UAL, United Airlines's parent company, closed on the New York Stock Exchange at $1.87 per share. Based on this share value, the market capitalization on that date of the largest airline in the world was $116.1 million—or roughly less than the cost of two Boeing 737s.

During the good years, corporate strategy was focused on luring the business traveler. By being able to charge outrageous fares to this customer segment, airlines were able to provide expensive conveniences that seemingly justified the prices that business travelers were paying. Schedules at hub-and-spoke airports provided passengers with flexibility in making their travel plans, something very important to the business traveler. Though such a system provided value to the customer, it also increased inefficiencies. Employees stood around between peak periods, planes sat on the ground longer and were prone to getting caught in line waiting to take off.

Despite the costs, such inefficiencies were acceptable while the airline industry and the U.S. economy were enjoying an unprecedented boom during the mid- to late 1990s. On most flights during this period, only a few first- and business-class passengers paying full fares were more than enough to offset the operating costs of all those economy class passengers in the back of the plane who were increasingly shopping on the Internet to get a better deal. However, when things slowed down in early 2001, the major airlines were caught in a minefield. Surrounding them were budget carriers like Southwest and Jet Blue that had lower operating overheads and the disaffection of millions of business passengers who were no longer willing to pay exorbitant fares.

Even before the 9/11 hijackings took place, the major carriers were already experiencing a threat to their fundamental business strategy. Months before the attacks, the number of business travelers began to evaporate as the economy slowed. In addition, those business passengers who continued to fly began to look for deals before booking their trips. Corporate travel managers were forcing the issue and making sure the number of two-thousand-dollar flights from Los Angeles to San Francisco were few and far between. It appeared the industry was slowing before those four planes were commandeered on September 11, 2001.

## TRYING TO MAKE SECURITY WORK

Air travel before the September 11 hijackings used to be a pretty straightforward, if not always pleasant, experience. Passengers might have felt queasy about the process of getting into the air, but such trepidations went pretty much dim once the plane was airborne. Except for the occasional bout with turbulence or a disruptive passenger, air travelers were for the most part able to predict, with a good degree of certainty, what their experience in the cabin would be like. It may not have been the most pleasant form of transportation, but air travel was certainly one of the most efficient and safest means for the vast majority of people. However, for millions of passengers, the searing images of 9/11 changed those views forever. How could anyone consider taking a trip and not think about the images of American Airlines flight 11 and United Airlines flight 175 slamming themselves into the World Trade Center towers?

Immediately after the attacks, airline stocks spiraled downward in a free fall. Passenger traffic dropped precipitously. The major carriers cut flight schedules and laid off thousands of employees. The future of the industry seemed to be hanging by a thread.

Restoring the public's confidence in the safety of the system after 9/11 was a top priority for all involved. In response, several measures were undertaken to demonstrate the resolve of the government to protect the nation's airports and passengers. Almost immediately after the attacks, President Bush called up the National Guard and ordered them stationed in airports across the country. Cockpit doors were ordered to be reinforced. Stricter standards at screening checkpoints were introduced.

The only problem is that these actions really didn't do a whole lot to improve security. The National Guard, which had never been involved in aviation security during its long history, was now asked to help passengers feel better simply by their mere presence. The cockpit door problem was still not solved. Placing two steel bars across the door from the inside was not enough to stop four disruptive passengers in separate incidents from getting into the cockpit even after 9/11. Meanwhile, taking away tens of thousands of nail clippers from passengers at checkpoints didn't do much to convince anybody that things were really significantly better than they were before the 9/11 attacks.

From the outset, the inability of the federal government to effectively manage the function of aviation security served as a major excuse for why air travel had slowed and remained sluggish many months after the 9/11 attacks. The "hassle factor," as it came to be known throughout the industry, was viewed as the primary reason passengers, and in particular business travelers, stayed away in droves from the nation's airports. The argument went that requiring someone to be at the airport two hours before their departure, negotiating long lines and waits at checkpoints, as well as being subjected to embarrassing searches and other exasperating security procedures had made air travel so burdensome and so time-consuming that a large percentage of the flying public began to choose another form of transportation or, instead, simply not travel at all. Passengers didn't want to be harassed with bans on curbside check-ins. It simply wasn't worth it. For millions of passengers, it seemed that security was a priority only as long as it didn't become an inconvenience.

## THE AIRLINES GO BACK UP TO CAPITOL HILL

In the weeks leading up to the first year anniversary of the 9/11 attacks, rumblings were felt throughout the industry that government-mandated security costs and inefficiencies were directly impacting the financial future of the airlines. Led by Leo Mullin, CEO of Delta, the airlines began to fight back, arguing that the government, not the airlines, should be responsible for preventing another September 11 from happening again.[5] In a speech to the

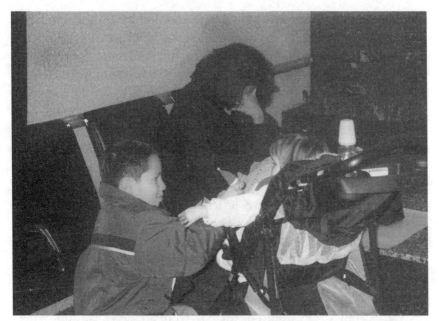

The "hassle factor," as it came to be known, was a major reason travelers were slow to come back to the skies after 9/11. Here, an exasperated mother and her children face more delays following a security breach at Cleveland's Hopkins International Airport.

Boston Chamber of Commerce, Mullin went so far to say that, "Without the impact of post–9/11 government policies, airlines would actually be posting a profit for 2002. While aviation security is *per se* better . . . in a painfully obvious case of unintended consequences, the challenge of security is producing a mountain of financial problems that nobody anticipated."[6]

Delta predicted that it would lose $700 million by the end of 2002. Erasing $600 million or more in security costs would significantly help that number, the company contended. First, the company claimed to have spent roughly $85 million after 9/11 to fortify cockpit doors, screen caterers, upgrade security at checkpoints, and buy new equipment—all costs mandated by the government. Further, executives of the airline argued that a September 11– related government clampdown on carrier shipments of mail and overnight packages had cost Delta about $90 million. According to corporate estimates, the airline was forced to absorb a $2.50 tax on each flight segment, or $5 on a round-trip ticket. For Delta, the cost generally added up to $10 per ticket, because connecting flights were charged the $2.50 as well and 70 percent of Delta passengers use a connecting flight. The ticket tax was supposed to be passed on to the consumer, but Delta contended the post–9/11 price slashing in the industry had left the major airlines powerless to raise ticket prices across the board.[7] At hearings on Capitol Hill during the fall of 2002, executives from Delta, American, Northwest, and Air Tran testified that most of the estimated $15 billion in industry losses were due to increased costs resulting from the 9/11 attacks.[8]

Carol Hallett, president of the Air Transport Association, when addressing what the airlines wanted from Congress said, "The airlines are not asking for a 'bailout.' We are not asking the federal government for special treatment. We are asking for recognition that government-imposed costs for the war on terrorism are seriously destabilizing the airline industry and threatening our broader transportation-dependent economy. The resulting rough estimate for the total post–9/11 security-related impact on the U.S. airline industry is about $4 billion."[9]

Included in the airlines' estimate was the new security tax of $2.50 per segment, which Congress presumed would be passed along to passengers. However, Hallett, like Delta's Mullin, said the airlines had to absorb the entire fee. "With available seats exceeding demand, it is instead falling to the airlines to cover this fee." In addition, Hallett added, "The airlines are also facing staggering increases in premiums for terrorism insurance (from $20 million in 2001 to $900 million in 2002); lost revenue due to new postal and air freight restrictions and other security requirements; nonreimbursed costs for cockpit door fortification; and government-imposed fees for passenger screening."[10] Sen. Peter Fitzgerald, who voted against the first airline bailout in 2001, said he was against this latest attempt by the airlines, which he said was "more cleverly disguised" than the previous year's bailout.[11]

While airline losses were estimated at about $7 billion in 2002, many questioned whether the airlines were really being impacted as much as they claimed by aviation security costs. For example, the ATSA mandated that airlines pay a fee that "may not exceed . . . the amounts paid in calendar year 2000 by carriers" for airport security screeners, training costs, and screening equipment. The airlines told the TSA during 2002 they spent about $300 million annually on security. But the DOT's Inspector General pointed out that the major airlines claimed before September 11, 2001—and testified twice afterward—that they spent between $750 million and $1 billion annually on security. Michael Wascom, spokesman for the Air Transport Association, said the $1 billion figure was only a rough estimate, and that it is difficult to tell how much is spent on security.[12]

Transportation Department spokesman Chet Lunner questioned whether the airlines' argument about security responsibilities beyond passenger screening were part of the deal. "We're just trying to collect what the Congress indicated was fair and equitable under the bill," Lunner said. The government was also disputing whether the airlines' figures were accurate, Lunner said.[13] The airlines later told the government that they would not pay the $750 million that the Transportation Security Administration had requested of them for the 2003 budget.[14]

Even more disconcerting, while the airlines were hemorrhaging billions, USA Today and the Center for Responsive Politics reported that the carriers still managed to give congressional candidates $4.1 million for the 2002 election. Despite the industry's dire finances, the industry's political spending for the 2002 election cycle was about the same as for the last nonpresidential election year, 1998, when airline profits were soaring. Moreover, during the first half of 2002, the industry spent $11.8 billion on lobbying in Washington.[15]

Beyond the questionable figures put forth by the airlines, many believed the industry's appeal for more federal aid was merely another attempt to cover up several self-inflicted wounds. Critics argued that the airlines' failure to control costs, principally labor, were often the difference between profit and loss. Several major carriers handed out fat raises to union workers as recently as the spring of 2001, even though they were already operating in the red. If US Airways, now in bankruptcy court, had labor costs as low as super-efficient Southwest, it would have turned a profit in the second quarter of 2002, according to an analysis by Standard and Poor's.[16]

In the end, despite the exaggerations on the part of the airlines, Congress seemed quite willing to come to the industry's assistance once again. The conventional wisdom on Capitol Hill seemed to emerge that although taxpayers have no responsibility to pay for an industry's failings, securing air travel is clearly a federal responsibility. And like other national security measures, the taxpayers must pay for it.

# CHAPTER 6
# CONCERNS ABOUT THE NEW AVIATION SECURITY SYSTEM

"When things go wrong, don't go with them."

—Elvis Presley

The Aviation and Transportation Security Act (ATSA) signed by President George W. Bush on November 19, 2001, promised a more seamless, sensible, and secure approach to protecting commercial aviation. Nevertheless, the view was held by many inside and outside of the industry that bad public policy and a lack of vision and leadership at the federal level delivered much less to the American people. Eighteen months after the 9/11 attacks, members of Congress, industry associations, independent experts, as well as most everyone else affected by the aviation sector were voicing loud concerns about the state of the new aviation security regimen.

Initially passed with the idea of making Americans feel better about their leaders and commercial aviation, ATSA would soon come to be one of the most criticized pieces of legislation in recent times. Almost immediately after the ink had dried from the president's numerous ballpoint pens signing the bill into law, skeptics began to slam ATSA.

## BIRTHPAINS AT TSA

The task of building a new federal agency in the midst of the greatest crisis in the history of commercial aviation was a daunting proposition at best. Trying to implement sweeping changes within the aviation security system while having to appease the airlines and reassure skittish passengers made short-term success a long shot. In the end, the first year of the TSA looked much more like the last one of the FAA. Bureaucratic inefficiency, relentless congressional pressure, and the power of market forces rose up to fight against the new agency's mission.

The individual thrust into the center of this whirlwind was John W. Magaw, former head of the Secret Service. When Magaw was sworn in as head of the TSA in January 2002, his powers were as wide-ranging as anybody's in the federal government. Representative John Mica, chairman of the House Transportation Committee told Magaw, "Congress has invested in you unprecedented executive authority . . . unlike anyone in the government except maybe the President." Mica added, "As far as I'm concerned, you don't need to check with Transportation Secretary Mineta or anybody else except maybe the President of the United States."[1]

The first step Magaw took was to surround himself with law enforcement people similar to himself. Most of the top officials at the TSA came from Secret Service, the Bureau of Alcohol, Tobacco, and Firearms, and state and local police agencies. Almost nobody with aviation security experience was brought into a high-level position. The one thousand or so mid-level civil aviation security specialists transferred from the FAA simply changed the agency for which they worked. Their new bosses consulted almost none of them on aviation security matters and they were left almost totally in the dark as to the mission and goals of the TSA.

According to a DOT analysis of the first months of the TSA, most of the agency's general and administrative positions were commanding salaries in excess of $90,000. As of July 27, 2002, TSA had hired 614 employees for nonscreener positions. Of these, 360—or 59 percent—had salaries higher than $90,000, while 269—or 44 percent—had salaries of more than $100,000. For example:

✗ Of the seventy-one employees hired in the General Inspection, Investigation, and Compliance series, fifty (70 percent) received annual salaries between $91,149 and $141,500.
✗ Of fifty criminal investigators hired, thirty-six (72 percent) had salaries ranging from $90,395 to $138,200.[2]

The lure of making more money working for the TSA caused a number of qualified employees already working for the federal government to leave the existing agencies and head off to the TSA. Offering raises of $10,000 or more to new recruits, TSA drained much-needed talent from the already struggling INS, and the Secret Service, U.S. Capitol Police, U.S. Park Police, and the FBI.[3]

In June 2002 it was widely reported that $410,000 had been spent to furnish TSA Chief Magaw's new office at DOT headquarters. The funds included money for mahogany-stained crown molding and doors, plush wall-to-wall carpeting, and a state-of-the-art conference room equipped with $109,000 worth of the latest high-tech audio and video equipment

Yet, despite spending nearly $6 billion in its first few months, many in the aviation sector and in Congress were beginning to think that the TSA was more dedicated to creating the agency itself that devising a system to improve aviation security. When airport managers around the country met for their national convention in May 2002, Magaw agreed to speak. The managers were quite relieved, thinking they were going to learn of TSA's plans for installing bomb-screening machines into their terminals and who was going to pay for it. But their expectations were never met. Magaw, aided by a big-screen display on the TSA's management structure, spent five minutes of his presentation on the development of the TSA logo. The basic bomb-screening questions were never addressed.[4]

A culture within the TSA was emerging that became increasingly insulated from the concerns of stakeholders within the aviation system. Calls from airport managers were not returned. Requests for clarifications from passenger groups were not responded to. And the media was becoming closed out of the inner workings of the agency. In this author's case, an initial telephone query was made to Greg Warren, a TSA spokesperson, in April 2002. After a cordial conversation, Warren suggested that any information being sought for this book be sent in writing. Agreeably, the author sent an e-mail request asking for clarification on the funding sources of TSA, including airline contributions, and the structure of TSA management at the nation's largest airports. None of the information asked for was classified and, moreover, not detrimental to the TSA's image. Two weeks went by without an answer. Finally, Mr. Warren left a voicemail message for the author saying that, "TSA did not think this book worthy of the agency and therefore would not assist the author in any way during his research."[5]

From the public's point of view, the agency seemed almost out of control. News reports emerged almost daily of little old ladies, decorated military veterans, John Glenn, Congressmen, and even Al Gore being shaken down at checkpoints now manned by TSA screeners or contractors. Mothers were forced to drink milk from their babies' bottles to be allowed through security. And, in May 2002, Blake Morrison of *USA Today* revealed that TSA screeners at thirty-two of the nation's largest airports failed to detect fake weapons—guns, dynamite, or bombs—in almost a quarter of the TSA's undercover tests. The tests, the first since the agency began overseeing checkpoint screening in February 2002, were conducted by agents who were instructed to do little to try to conceal the items as they passed through screening checkpoints.[6] Amidst the flurry of bad press and growing concern that the TSA was going to miss the December 31, 2002, baggage-screening deadline, John Magaw quit in July 2002 and was replaced by Admiral James Loy, former head of the U.S. Coast Guard. And so ended the first months of the government's attempt to secure America's aviation system. Without any praise and with a feeling of insecurity still in the air.

## OLD WINE IN NEW BOTTLES

Much of the fault-finding centered on the TSA operating under the Department of Transportation (DOT). A top official in the Bush administration working in counterterrorism policy said a week after the new law went into effect, "There's been no meaningful changes. DOT is a front for the airlines. They don't do law enforcement. I proposed they move security over to the U.S. Marshals or have the Department of Justice set it up as an independent organization. But it obviously didn't sell."[7]

Steve Elson, a former FAA special agent and member of the agency's elite Red Team, called the new legislation "old wine in new bottles." Elson noted, "The law keeps the aviation security organization under Transportation, where the airlines and other moneyed interests can control it. FAA agents in the field say they're being told their jobs are safe, and that they can really just expect just a name change."[8]

Sen. Conrad Burns, a Republican from Montana, was another of those who questioned the new TSA being placed within the DOT. Even though he supported the final version of the ATSA bill, Burns admitted later on the floor of the Senate that Congress "took a wrong turn" when it decided not to put airline security under the Department of Justice. "Who deals with security every day and has the experience to do it? Who can best be put to work the quickest and have people on the ground doing the business the fastest, without creating a new bureaucracy? . . . This was not allowed to be discussed in conference. . . . There was no debate, so the American people were not given a real choice between a new bureaucracy and a bureaucracy that is already in place."[9]

Ironically, almost a year later, Magaw concurred. "It really boils down to that they [Congress] put it [TSA] in the wrong place. That's not a criticism of the Department of Transportation; it's just not their cup of tea."[10]

Even before the legislation passed, the airlines were concerned that taking a look at every checked bag would inconvenience passengers and burden airports to the point of greatly reducing air travel in the United States. The pressure on Congress began to build. On November 7, 2001, Donald Carty, CEO of American Airlines, warned of job cuts and reduced service if bag matching was mandated. "We're talking about more airline layoffs, we're talking about downsizing of airlines, we're talking about inconvenienced customers. We're talking about a system that will do nothing about the kind of incident that occurred on September 11."[11] Leo Mullin, Delta's CEO in a November 14 speech to the New York Wings Club predicted "revenue losses as high as $3.5 billion" if the airline were forced into passenger bag matching.[12]

In the final version of the bill, under Section 110, the TSA was directed to provide for "screening" of all passengers and property, including checked baggage that would be carried aboard a passenger aircraft operated by an airline. This did not mean that every bag would have to be searched or run through a bomb detection machine. Instead, using one of several possible methods—some of them deliberately vague—the TSA could insure that checked baggage was secure and screened before entering the cargo hold of an aircraft. Within sixty days, all checked baggage at all airports in the United States was to be "screened." That is, deemed secure to travel. Whatever that meant.

Where explosives detection machines were not available, alternative means of screening available to the TSA consisted of:

✈ A bag-match program that ensured no checked baggage would go aboard unless the passenger who checked it was on board

✈ Manual searches of checked luggage

✈ Canine explosives detection in combination with other means

✈ Technology approved by the TSA

So in essence, the TSA was given an incredible amount of latitude to meet a key provision of the new law. The TSA was required to take all necessary action to ensure that explosives detection machines were deployed as soon as possible to make sure all airports could screen all bags no later than December 31, 2002. All available machines were to be fully used. However, if enough machines were not available by then, alternative means could still be used. In the vague and uncertain language of the new aviation bill, the Congress had once again deferred to the DOT and the airline industry when it came to protecting the safety of the flying public.

For many observers, the proof of "old wine in new bottles" was evident a few weeks later when the 2002 Aviation Issues Conference was held at the Hapuna Beach Prince Hotel in Kona, Hawaii. From January 6–10, 2002, among the palm trees, pristine beaches, and breathtaking golf courses of a tropical wonderland, government officials, airline executives, and airport directors mingled to discuss the future of the industry.

The conference was sponsored by forty-six separate entities. Many of the major airlines and their trade associations were there. So were several Washington-based lobbying firms who worked on behalf of the industry's efforts on Capitol Hill. The major manufacturers, including Boeing, Airbus, and Lockheed Martin were well represented as well as the interests of airports and airport executives. In addition, several of the firms already doing business or hoping to do business with the government in the area of aviation security technology helped to defray the expenses of the conference. It seemed anyone who was anybody in the industry was there.

Also, according to the *Washington Post*, "eight members of Congress and dozens of Senate and House aides were expected to attend."[13] Included in the government entourage was to be Senate Minority Leader Tom Daschle, husband of airline lobbyist Linda Daschle. There were even hopes that Kenneth Mead, Inspector General of the DOT, the agency's top watchdog, would be able to make an appearance.[14]

Besides mai tais, mulligans, and moonlit strolls on the beach, surely one of the most vexing issues confronting conference attendees was the baggage screening requirements that were an integral component of ATSA. Even before the legislation had passed, the industry was hard at work pushing for changes. Just before Congress adjourned for the Christmas recess, there were reports that the industry was hard at work lobbying key members to amend portions of the new law that dealt with checked baggage. Most certainly, this had to be a hot topic of poolside discussion in Hawaii.

## WHAT HAPPENED TO ALL THE MONEY?

In late 2002, the agency announced it had spent $6 billion and was borrowing funds from another federal agency. "I have to remind members what we did to create the TSA monster," Representative John Mica said at a House Committee on Transportation and Infrastructure. "We created the monster and we've got to get it under control." Lou Tyska, chairman of the transportation security committee for the American Society for Industrial Security, a trade group of corporate security chiefs, observed that the TSA "was overwhelmed, understaffed, and wrongly positioned to accomplish everything that was thrown at them. . . . They were doomed to failure."[15]

When it came down to funding the agency, more money never seemed quite enough. Secretary of Transportation Norman Mineta testified on Capitol Hill on July 23, 2002, that because the agency couldn't get any more money, TSA was going to have to stop much of what it was doing.

> Today I was expecting to discuss TSA's challenges, to seek your counsel, report to you on what is working, and tell you what needs improving. But the extraordinary delay in approving emergency funding and new restrictions imposed on TSA have dramatically undermined our ability to meet this goal. Four months ago, President Bush asked Congress to approve a $4.4 billion Emergency Supplemental Bill to stand up this new agency. That is a lot of money, but that should not be surprising because the mandates set out in the TSA legislation are ambitious.
>
> In the meantime, TSA borrowed money, renegotiated payment schedules with our vendors, deferred purchase of explosives detection equipment, and set back the pilot testing of various security measures. Now TSA is literally days away from running out of money to pay for the ongoing work of screeners nationwide. Less money with no flexibility means fewer TSA employees, less equipment, longer lines, delay in reducing the hassle factor at airports, and/or diminished security at our nation's airports. Frankly, these conflicting signals sent by Congress have forced us to regroup and revise the TSA business plan. That will likely take several more weeks. It will involve complex negotiations, and a review of literally thousands of TSA commitments and plans.[16]

The high salaries of the new agency's employees notwithstanding, the TSA also spent billions of dollars on outside contracts that were questionable both in their amounts and who was awarded them. Lockheed Martin was brought in to train checkpoint screeners and upgrade screening checkpoints at the nation's 429 commercial airports. In phase one of the Lockheed Martin contract, valued at $105 million, the defense contractor agreed to establish training centers local to each airport; ensure that each screener received forty-four hours of classroom instruction; and, provide final exams as a graduation requirement. In phase two, the firm was to begin airport passenger-lane reconfiguration and implement technologies at security checkpoints at the nation's airports. The base value of that contract was $350 million.

The Lockheed Martin contracts were of particular interest because of the options on 18,400 shares of Lockheed stock held by the Transportation secretary. Secretary Mineta, a former Lockheed vice president who left the company in 2000 to become President Clinton's Commerce secretary, retained options to purchase the shares after joining the government.[16] Further, during the 2000–2001 election cycle, Lockheed Martin gave more than $2.7 million in political action committee (PAC), soft money, and individual donations to House and Senate members from both parties on Capitol Hill.[17]

Boeing was contracted to assess other airport facilities, submit design plans, and make needed improvements to meet the requirements of the ATSA. The contract, valued at $508 million, paid Boeing for the installation of up to eleven hundred explosives detection systems and between forty-eight hundred and six thousand explosives trace detection machines in the nation's airports.[18] It also provided training for a minimum of 21,500 federal baggage screeners to operate the equipment. Of course, the machines and personnel had to be paid for by somebody else. This contract was only the first step. Also, it may be noteworthy to point out that during the 2000–2001 election cycle, Boeing gave nearly $2 million in PAC, soft money, and individual donations to House and Senate members from both parties on Capitol Hill.[19]

Charles Slepian of the Foreseeable Risk Assessment Center in New York and a leading critic of the new aviation security apparatus, pointed out that in addition to the DOT rewarding some of the largest contributors on Capitol Hill with contracts, the nature of the contracts themselves was dubious. Slepian explained that the largest contracts with the TSA had been parceled out to subcontractors, often resulting in greater difficulty in evaluating the performance of the contractors themselves.

According to Slepian,

> Lockheed Martin's program for training airport screeners is one example. Lockheed apparently subcontracted out its duties to a company called Homeland Security Inc., whose origins are unclear as are its ties to Lockheed and its assigned duties. Homeland Security, Inc. evidently purchased another company called PPCT, which for many years trained law enforcement personnel on the use of force issues. PPCT apparently used its contacts with law enforcement agencies from around the country to recruit instructors to train the TSA's new screeners. Another group of companies, some in the security business and some likely created for purposes of implementing the original Lockheed contract, recruited still other trainers from law enforcement to provide a training cadre.
>
> The terms of the hiring of these personnel and their status as independent contractors doing work for the Federal Government provides, at the very least, an appearance of possible impropriety. Many of those hired in these training capacities, or as training managers for the nation's airports, have been assigned little work, and have been paid at different wage rates for similar work. Further, some have been dismissed after short periods of employment for similar work, and some have been dismissed after short periods of employment without explanation, despite the expenditure of large sums of taxpayer dollars to train them. In short, the management of taxpayer dollars now in the hands of some of the contractors requires accounting for. And, the hiring and firing practices of these personnel employed to carry out functions being undertaken on behalf of the United States government likewise needs to be audited.[20]

## SCATTERSHOT SOLUTIONS

On the eve of the first anniversary of the 9/11 attacks, *USA Today* observed that "the Transportation Security Administration had adopted a scattershot approach, starting many tasks, completing few." The editorial went on to say, "The TSA still lacks a priority list of doable projects, realistic timetables, the will to stick to them—and the candor to acknowledge errors and delays."[21]

The International Air Cargo Association (TIACA)—the Miami-based trade group representing the airlines and air freight shippers—criticized the TSA for implementing what it called a "patchwork" of costly security measures that are not effective in preventing future attacks. Specifically, TIACA centered its concerns on the ability of an explosive device or weapon of mass destruction to be placed in the belly of an aircraft. TIACA president Larry Coyne said that "while the reaction to September 11 was understandable, some of the measures introduced were not. We must therefore ask if all this money is being used to buy effective security. Unfortunately, since many of the measures have been rushed without due consideration, we are not getting the best value for our money."[22]

Concern about the TSA's overemphasis on technology was also voiced. Isaac Yeffet, the former El Al security chief, has maintained that the focus of aviation security has always tended to focus too much on technology rather than on well-trained and well-educated human beings. "You deal with sophisticated terrorists today. You can't even dream of a machine that gives you all the answers. But a human being will give you the answers."[23]

Philip Baum, editor of *Aviation Security International* magazine, said much of the industry was still too reliant on technology to battle against the threats to aviation. "For as long as we rely on technology alone, the events of September 11 will be able to be repeated by the terrorists around the world. Metal detectors and X-ray machines were OK in the '60s and '70s, but they can't pick up small blades, or knives made out of plastic or some other substance."[24]

A long-standing criticism of aviation security policy in the United States is that the last major attack on the system tends to drive the implementation of new security measures. The view holds that we are continually fighting the last war and allowing the perpetrators of violence to educate us about the vulnerabilities of the system. Throughout the thirty-year history of aviation security, almost all of the substantive security improvements have come in direct response to a particular incident. For many, the key to providing comprehensive and workable security is to project beyond the last attack and look to what future scenarios may be. Chris Yates, editor of London-based *Jane's Civil Aviation Security,* said that even after the creation of the TSA, the public was still in danger from terrorists targeting air travel. Yates said most security efforts concentrated on preventing another round of suicide hijackings, to the neglect of other, potentially more likely terror scenarios.[25]

Other concerns were raised about the law enforcement and military focus of the TSA. Historically, principles of law enforcement and military practice have not been transferable to practice within the private sector. Many contended that TSA didn't have the capacity to understand how to operate within an environment made up of businesses like airlines and airports that were driven by market forces, not bureaucratic missions. Critics said the TSA was born out of a law enforcement culture with a large number of former Secret Service and law enforcement officials. This culture, they said, fueled the agency's rapidly growing interpretation of its duties as more of a traditional law enforcement organization than a security agency.

Original projections called for the TSA to employ about twenty-eight thousand airport screeners. But the DOT's inspector general now predicts there will be more than seventy thousand TSA employees by the end of 2003. Airports complained that the TSA was stretching its authority into their turf. The TSA wants to oversee security around airport perimeters, such as areas where trucks carrying airline meals and cargo gain access to the tarmac—

space that airports see as their responsibility. After the fatal shootings of July 4, 2002, by an Egyptian immigrant at a Los Angeles International Airport ticket counter, the TSA first said it was responsible for security only at security checkpoints. The next day, however, the agency said it would place armed federal officers in terminal lobbies. Two weeks later, however, the TSA backed off.[26]

## ANOTHER DUAL MANDATE?

As time wore on, many inside and outside Washington were becoming increasingly concerned that the TSA was beginning to repeat the same mistakes as its predecessor—the FAA—when it came to balancing the needs of the industry with the demand for security. From its beginnings, the TSA was to be a law enforcement organization, but one that included customer service as part of its mission. Transportation Secretary Mineta's search for an official with a strong law enforcement background to head the agency led to John Magaw, a former head of the Secret Service who had rebuilt the Bureau of Alcohol, Tobacco, and Firearms following its ill-fated encounter with the Branch Davidian sect in Waco, Texas, in 1993. But many argued that Magaw ignored the service aspect of the agency as he assembled the TSA.

Following Magaw's resignation, Mineta restated before Congress that, "We have a customer service orientation that we have to deal with as well as safety and security. The way to build confidence in the [aviation] system is to be able to move goods and people safely. And at the same time, people want to make sure they won't have to wait two hours to get something done."[27] But as with the FAA, the great question remained: how could TSA balance the needs of the industry with the responsibility of insuring the safety and security of that same industry?

To become more customer service oriented, the agency borrowed a crowd-management specialist from Disney World to

Passenger checkpoints were the primary focus of the new Transportation Security Administration. Borrowing techniques used by Disney theme parks, the TSA sought to provide travelers with both "world-class security and world-class service." Many wondered if this wasn't eerily similar to the dual mandate of the TSA's predecessor: the Federal Aviation Administration.

study the ways in which passengers approach screening stations, and how they interact with security personnel. At Baltimore/ Washington International Airport, a pilot program based on a Disney design was put into place. Instead of forcing passengers to stand in a single line that snakes through the airport, travelers now stand in switchbacks that will be familiar to riders of amusement park roller coasters. Flat-panel television monitors tell passengers what to expect and offer tips on how to be better prepared when they reach the security screens. The televised instructions tell air-

DO NOT ENTER

The TSA was the largest federal agency created since World War II. More than seventy thousand federal employees were hired to upgrade the level of security for the nation's airports after 9/11, at a cost of over $8 billion. Whether aviation security is any better with the TSA in control remains an open question.

port visitors to take metal objects out of their pockets and put them into carry-ons for screening. The screens advise passengers in advance to take laptops out of cases and prepare to put them in special screening bins. They are further advised to remove their coats before getting to the X-ray machines. The advice prepares passengers for what they are about to experience, thus speeding the processing time. One machine is dedicated to screening shoes alone. Security runners take passengers' shoes to the machines while those passengers go through other security procedures. Chairs are set aside to allow passengers to put their shoes back on while staying out of the way of those who follow.

In addition, TSA chief James Loy announced the agency was going to do away with several "stupid rules," as he called them. Random gate screenings, a procedure that was implemented after the 9/11 attacks, were eliminated. The agency also got rid of the policy that prohibited passengers from carrying liquids, like cups of coffee and bottles of water, through checkpoints. Loy said that the changing of these policies was designed to increase customer service and eliminate the hassle factor experienced by passengers.[28]

Although almost nobody would question the need to efficiently move passengers through screening checkpoints, doubts remained if Loy's changes didn't ultimately compromise security. In August 2002, a woman carrying a loaded .357 Magnum on a Delta flight from Atlanta was detected with the weapon in her carry-on during a random gate search as she tried to board a connecting flight in Philadelphia. In FBI reports released the week before Loy's announcement, the TSA and airlines were warned of a possible Al Qaeda plot to hijack a plane using liquid explosives mixed with coffee.

The airline industry, however, was unwavering in its support for Loy and his desire to make things easier and more passenger friendly. The checks on passengers and stops and searches meant long lines and inconvenience for passengers. And that cut into profits. Michael Wascom, spokesperson for the Air Transport Association, said, "Our input was not always welcomed in the early days of the TSA. Loy has been much more receptive to at least understanding our ideas. Now we're happy. We're much happier than we were a few months ago."[29]

# PART 2

# A NEW SET OF EYES

Criticism simply for the sake of criticism is the purview of only a select few. Those who critique books, movies, plays, and restaurants, for example, do so knowing full well that the veracity of their criticism only goes as far as their personal tastes. In the commercial world, such an approach to criticism is anathema. If someone seeks to criticize a particular business strategy or tactic, they darn well better have a viable alternative. If they don't, they had better step aside.

Part I of this book was the author's attempt at criticism of the post–9/11 aviation security regimen. The remainder of this book is his endeavor to look at aviation security in a different and fresh way. If you continue to repeat the same mistakes over and over . . . well, you know the rest.

If 9/11 has taught us anything, it is that our approach to aviation security prior to the attacks was gravely flawed. Even more disconcerting, however, is the fact that instead of trying to learn from our past mistakes, it appears the concept of aviation security today is eerily familiar to that of pre-9/11.

What we had before 9/11 and even today, I would argue, is a scattershot of countermeasures. Some work, some don't, but we never really

*seem to understand how any of this impacts the overall protection of avi-
ation. We haven't taken the time to see how these countermeasures—the
good ones as well as the bad ones—interact with the other aspects of the
aviation security system. And there's the key word: system . . .*

# CHAPTER 7

# RISK ANALYSIS AND AVIATION SECURITY

"Bad security looks a lot like good security on the surface."

—Anonymous

Security in its purest form can be defined as the state that is achieved when a stable and safe system exists, in which individuals or groups can pursue their ends and objectives without disruption or harm and without fear of loss or injury. Broadly speaking, a security system is designed to keep people from creating problems or hurting people or property. Security, therefore, is a condition that results from the establishment and maintenance of a system that ensures protection against violation from hostile acts or influences.

Since its creation in early 2002, the TSA has poorly practiced what has long been the approach to security in the industry—the idea of layered security. The concept of layered security is not unique to aviation; it is used in a wide variety of settings and industries. The principle of layered security is rooted in the notion that the failure of a single layer of security does not mean the entire system will be breached. Such a strategy is purposefully designed to put enough obstacles in the way of perpetrators of violence that they will be deterred from trying to attack the system. And, even if they persist, multiple breaches would have to take place for them to be successful. In theory, layered security increases the likelihood of failure for a potential perpetrator of violence against the system. Consequently, only the most foolhardy, deranged, or hostile individual or group would even try to embark on such a task.

Despite how it reads on paper, the practice of layered security that was in place on September 11, 2001, was miserably defective. The terrorists were successful on that day because they had to breach up to three poorly designed layers of security. It really wasn't that hard for them to do.

Let's remember that between nine and eleven hijackers had been selected for further screening by a sophisticated computer-profiling system prior to boarding their flights. The Computer Assisted Passenger Screening System (CAPS) that was in place on 9/11 detected that many of the hijackers had purchased their one-way tickets with cash, setting off red flags. Unfortunately, that particular layer of security on 9/11 mandated a thorough search of only a profiled passenger's checked luggage—not their carry-ons or their persons. Since most of the hijackers had no checked luggage, no further scrutiny was performed on them.

A second layer, the checkpoint screening process, was so ill-prepared for the 9/11 attacks that the known weapons of choice for the hijackers—box cutters—were actually legal to carry onboard commercial aircraft. If the terrorists hadn't wanted to take the chance of raising any suspicions, though box cutters were legal, they could have easily purchased similar items at kiosks or retail stores after they went through the security checkpoint. On the off chance that there were no box cutters available, they could have ordered a steak at a restaurant before departing and asked for a larger knife. I did this in Cleveland at a restaurant the week before the attacks while traveling with my son. The steak knife the waitress brought me was approximately six inches long with a strong metal handle. I could have easily eaten my steak, placed my napkin over the plate when I was finished, and put the knife in my bag or pocket. By the time the staff working in the busy restaurant ever realized their knife was missing, I would have been long gone.

The third porous layer was the flimsy cockpit door. Despite more than two dozen cockpit intrusions in the twenty-four months leading up to the attacks, nothing was done to make the door sturdier to withstand an attack. The original design for the door was meant for easy egress from the cockpit for the crew in the event of an emergency evacuation. Not a lot of engineering nor planning went into keeping people from entering through the cockpit door.

Once those layers were breached, nothing stood in the terrorists' way of carrying out their mission. There were no other countervailing or layered security measures in place that would have stopped them. In fact, there were policies in place on 9/11 that might actually have assisted the terrorists in breachng these layers. FAA directives that required flight attendants to carry a key to the cockpit door on their person gave the terrorists a means of breaching that thin layer of security. Attack a flight attendant, grab their key, unlock the door, and walk into the cockpit. In addition, airline policies that encouraged the captain or copilot to leave the cockpit in the event of an in-cabin disturbance further provided the hijackers with another way of getting through the door. Create an incident in the back of the plane as a diversion; wait for one of the crew to exit the cockpit; and, at that moment, neutralize him or her and walk through the opened door.

In response to what happened on 9/11, the TSA set out to put as many impediments as possible in the way of potential terrorists so that the events of that fateful day could not be repeated. Still adhering to the theory and practice of layered security, aviation security planners sought to make it much more daunting to hijack an aircraft and fly it into a predetermined target on the ground. The idea was twofold. First, it increased the sheer number of layers of security that future terrorists would have to negotiate. Second, it gave those layers more strength and depth. This way we will dramatically reduce the likelihood of another 9/11-type attack.

To be blunt, however, this strategy missed the mark. Simply adding more layers without regard to an assessment of the overall effectiveness of those new layers does not increase security. Bad security systems look like good ones on the outside. It is only when we view them as an integrated whole that we are able to see if the job of securing the system is truly being accomplished.

The following is a cursory analysis of the layered security approach in place today that is designed to prevent another 9/11-style hijacking:

### Layer #1: Higher Screening Standards

The TSA continues to proclaim that the standards for screening have become much stricter, although new reports reveal that large numbers of prohibited items get through checkpoints.

### Layer #2: Increased Profiling

The TSA also promises that by using the newer, more advanced version of the Computerized Assisted Passenger Screening System (CAPS II), more and more individuals that may be possible threats are chosen by computer selection and subjected to greater scrutiny and intensive searches of their person and their luggage—including both carry-ons and checked bags.

### Layer #3: Better Screening at Checkpoints

Even if a potential terrorist is not selected by CAPS II and he nonetheless tries to sneak a prohibited item past a checkpoint, the new, better-trained, better-paid, and better-motivated federal employees are purportedly much more likely to detect the potential weapon than the private sector security screeners of the past.

*Layer #4: Reinforced Cockpit Doors*

Assuming the potential terrorist could somehow smuggle a gun or a long-edged knife past a checkpoint, the TSA claims that the reinforced cockpit door will supposedly keep any potential hijacker out and prevent him from turning the plane into a flying missile.

*Layer #5: Air Marshals*

With more air marshals now traveling on more flights, the TSA asserts that the chances are increased that a well-trained marshal will be able to take out a potential hijacker long before he can work his way into the cockpit door.

*Layer #6: Armed Pilots*

In the very remote chance a hijacker manages to get through the cockpit door and an air marshal is not on board, there is the greater possibility that one of the pilots will be armed and trained to shoot the hijacker and stop the plane from being taken over.

*Layer #7: Passenger Action*

In the event there is no air marshal on board and neither one of the pilots is carrying a firearm and a terrorist manages to pierce the door, passengers and flight crew will ultimately intervene and take down the hijackers as they did on United flight 93 (though at the cost of their own lives).

*Layer #8: Shoot-down Policy*

Finally, if all of the other layers fail, F-15 and F-16 fighters are standing by at military bases across the country waiting for the call to scramble and, if necessary, shoot down a hijacked aircraft before it can become a flying weapon of mass destruction.

According to the theory of layered security as it has been practiced in the past, with all of these new layers now in place, the likelihood of a 9/11-type attack should be almost zero. Instead of three weak layers of security in place as there were on 9/11, there are now most certainly six, and quite possibly eight, layers in place—depending on whether an air marshal or armed pilot are on the plane. Therefore, only the most imprudent or demented individual would now try to do what the terrorists did on 9/11. The system has been secured as well as it can be and the layered security approach has worked.

Unfortunately, this is not quite true—especially given the current operating environment. Let's look at how a terrorist thinks. If I am a trained killer—a terrorist—I am not concerned about any weapon (including an air marshal's or a pilot's) being used against me, for the chances of that happening are slim to none. When I enter the airport, I do not need to carry anything on my person or in my luggage that a computer-selected search or alert checkpoint screener might detect.

The new fortified cockpit doors will prevent low-grade hijackers and air rage perpetrators from invading the cockpit by breaking through the door, but they do nothing to deter the well-trained, determined terrorist. If I am that person, I know that I do not have to break through the cockpit door. Leave that to the amateurs. All I have to do is occupy a seat toward the front of the plane and rush the cockpit door when it is open. The next time you're on a plane, count the number of times the cockpit door is open during your flight and for how long. It is a virtual certainty that at some point a flight attendant will knock on the door and it will be opened or the pilot or copilot will rise to exit the door to use the lavatory. That's when I would make my move.

If a flight attendant is blocking my way through the door, I'll hit him or her with a solid body check and send him or her flying, probably into the pilot who unlocked the door from the inside. On some carriers, I've noticed that a flight attendant or two will gather with their serving carts in front of the cockpit before the door is open to try to block me. No problem there. I'll simply push the carts back onto the flight attendants and jump through their "blockade." Either way, before anyone can even think of reacting, I am in the cockpit and my training enables me to incapacitate or kill anybody in there in short order with my bare hands. Even if there is an air marshal on board who is awake and alert, he has little or no opportunity to stop me. I have moved so quickly that I am inside the cockpit before he can draw his firearm. The same with an armed pilot or copilot. It has all happened so fast that nobody has had time to react.

By the time the air marshal has reacted, I have locked the bulletproof door behind me and he has no way of reaching me. I have reached this point without the help of accomplices, without a weapon, and with little or no resistance, because I have planned this very carefully and know there is no way to defend against me. I have moved much too quickly and forcefully for anyone to even contemplate resisting, and am now in complete control. Now I have a perfect fortress all to myself so I can do as I please. By the time the fighter jets are scrambled and take off after me, I'm already well on the way to slamming my plane into a chemical plant, an office tower, or almost any other target I desire. There is nothing that can stop me.

I am using the layered security theory against itself, and it works for me much better than it worked for the pilots. Layered security did not protect them, but it now protects me. Did the presence of an air marshal or an armed pilot make any difference at all, except to make everyone more complacent? Now, unlike the pilots, I will not make the mistake of opening the cockpit door for anyone who knocks.

If I am a hijacker, I will fly only an aircraft that opens the cockpit door during flight. That is the only time I am interested in that door, when some unsuspecting person opens it for me. I don't even have to open it for myself. Funny how almost everything is done for me. All I have to do is get the timing right, and the rest is easy. I know exactly how to exploit weaknesses in the system, and the consequences can be catastrophic.[1]

The new layers of security, including the fortified cockpit door, will, if not completely thought all the way through, make hijacking much easier for the trained terrorist. In the past, hijackers boarded aircraft in groups of five or more, and it was the duty of several of them to prevent passengers from attacking those who commandeered the cockpit. With the new fortified door there is little need for the group approach, as there is no need to control the passengers.

One person gaining entry to the cockpit can lock out everyone else, and he needs no help. All the help he needs is already built into the aircraft; it is simply a matter of using that to his advantage. A single, unarmed hijacker can now take over the largest aircraft, and do so at little risk to himself.

Everything they need will be provided for them by their victims, as it was on 9/11. Despite all the layers, we have actually made the terrorists' job of hijacking an aircraft and turning it into a flying missile easier in quite a number of ways.

What we see in this example is the very real difference between security theory and security practice. Security theory—in this case the layered approach—fails in practice because it doesn't take into account other factors that have been either missed or ignored by the designers. As Yogi Berra said, "In theory there is no great difference between theory and practice. In practice there is." Despite all of the new measures put in place, the layered security theory fails because it never recognizes that every door is vulnerable every time it is opened. This means that the door has to be defended from the outside, not from within the cockpit. Once the door is breached there is no possibility of repelling a well-planned attack.

From this scenario there are several lessons, or realities, that can be drawn. They provide insight into better understanding how to approach aviation security—in practice—in the post 9/11 environment:

*Reality #1: The aviation security system*
*is only as strong as its weakest point.*

This may sound trite, but it is true. Despite all of the new measures put in place to prevent a hijacker from getting into the cockpit of an aircraft, the system in this example was unable to prevent the breach because a single part of the system (controlling the opening and closing of the door during flight) allowed a real threat to successfully exploit a previously unaddressed vulnerability. If the cockpit door was always closed, along with all the other layers that were put in place, then the opposite would be true. The likelihood of a 9/11-type attack would be negligible.

*Reality #2: Aviation will always be attacked.*

As you are reading this article, criminal activity is taking place right now on board an aircraft or at an airport somewhere in the world. A disruptive passenger on a present flight is acting up and threatening the safety of passengers and flight crew. And a terrorist group is drawing up plans to hit the aviation system once again at a weak point. It is simply a fact of life that aviation has and always will serve as an attractive target for criminals and terrorists, as well as a forum for the bad behavior of disruptive passengers.

*Reality #3: The aviation system is complex*
*and getting even more so every day.*

The reason it is increasingly difficult to secure something as complex as the aviation system is because of the system's intrinsic complexity. As the most global of all transportation systems, the scope and magnitude of air transport is truly remarkable. Each year, more than 1.5 billion passengers and several billion tons of cargo are moved from every corner of the world. They are transported on more than twenty-five thousand commercial airliners, which operate from more than fifteen hundred commercial airports around the globe. The scale of the system is immense and so are its complexities.

*Reality #4: Magic bullets are never the answer.*

Throughout its history, most approaches to aviation security have focused on one or a few "magic bullets" (i.e. air marshals, reinforced cockpit doors, armed pilots, shoot-down policies), rather than an entire system. These magic bullets are characteristically easy to implement for planners, simple to explain to the public, and compatible with the industry's needs for convenience and customer service. By failing to address the needs of the entire system, however, most vulnerabilities have remained woefully unaddressed. Moreover, you can bet attacks on those vulnerabilities will be high probabilities.

*Reality #5: Technology does not provide us a fail-safe system; processes do.*

Technology most certainly has its place within the framework of aviation security. However, relying almost exclusively on technology fails to recognize the human element in both attacking the system as well as preventing, detecting, and responding to those potential attacks. Even the most advanced computer profiling system cannot read someone's body language. If the potential perpetrator does nothing on the outside to reveal his intentions, there had better be human countermeasures and processes in place to thwart the attack. Processes are the ways human beings protect what is important to them. Technology is merely one way to help make that happen.

*Reality #6. Aviation security measures often do things
we didn't expect them to do.*

In the example of the fortified cockpit door, the designers of the
door as well as the door's users probably never expected that the
door could be used against them. As a rule, unintended consequences of an aviation security measure must always be planned
for and counted on to happen.

In the realm of aviation, the "doing" of security is provided by
a wide range of organizations that work on behalf of the flying
public and the many stakeholders that are affected by the system.
Local police departments, airlines, airports, and others—all under
the direction and authority of the TSA—contribute substantially to
the delivery of aviation security. The coordination of these entities
into one, singular security-oriented team operating within the
physical infrastructure of the aviation industry is the foundation of
the system. The remainder of this book will concentrate on
explaining why aviation security must be looked at in a systemic
way and how that system should function and operate.

# RISK ANALYSIS AND AVIATION SECURITY

Risk analysis has historically been used throughout the business
world to identify systematically the risks within a specified environment and ensure that appropriate processes commensurate with
the risks are implemented and managed. A risk analysis, in the clas-
sical sense, is a process that an organization goes through to determine its risk exposure. Risk is the possibility that damage could be
inflicted upon a system. The goal of a risk analysis is to determine
the probability of potential risks in order to reasonably integrate
security tactics and methods to effectively manage those risks.

Risk is everywhere. It is all around us. In the bathtub, on the drive home, in our food. Risk is an uncertainty that affects our welfare, and is most often associated with loss or hardship. Since risk is an inevitability to living our lives and there is no way we can get away from it, we try our best to manage it. We put rubber mats on the floor of the bathtub to get better traction. We wear seatbelts. We try to make sure that food is clean and properly cooked before we eat it. However, despite our efforts to manage risk, we have to accept that it still exists.

In aviation, like all other human endeavors, ascertained risk is managed risk. Generally speaking, when we establish the amount of risk in a given situation and implement ways to reduce the uncertainty surrounding it, we ultimately lower the level of risk associated with the event. Consequently, managing risk involves choosing among various alternatives to reduce the effects of risk.

Managing risk is *not* avoiding it. Instead, it involves finding the best available combination of risk and return given a system's capacity to withstand the effects of risk. Effective risk management involves anticipating outcomes as well as planning strategy and tactics in advance given their likelihood, not merely reacting to those events after they occur. At its core, managing risk is proactive.

The idea of managing risk within the aviation industry flies in the face of traditional notions of security, especially those practiced historically. The traditional method of protecting the aviation system has been based upon implementing more and more countermeasures as the way to manage risk. Crudely stated, such an approach to security follows the line of reasoning that, "If we throw enough countermeasures against the wall, a certain number will stick which will somehow make us more secure."

After 9/11, security planners increased the number of air marshals, deployed National Guardsmen at airports, implemented a shoot-down policy, reinforced cockpit doors, and a number of other measures, all with the goal of eliminating threats. The problem is that eliminating threats happens or it doesn't. Either the threat is dodged or it is not. It is very black or very white. And it leaves little or no room for error.

In order to get more air marshals up in the skies after 9/11, the twelve-week training of new air marshal recruits used in the past was dramatically cut to only six weeks. Consequently, instead of having a well-disciplined force patrolling the skies, we saw in several instances that the new air marshals were not much more than vigilantes with guns who too often lacked the knowledge to operate within the confines of an aircraft cabin.

Deploying National Guardsmen at the nation's airports for nearly nine months after 9/11 cost billions of dollars and did nothing to significantly improve aviation security. National Guardsmen, despite all of their valiant efforts, know next to nothing about aviation security and even less about the real threats to and vulnerabilities of the system.

The shoot-down policy implemented after 9/11 has put almost a dozen airliners in jeopardy of being mistakenly shot down because of the simple fact that F-15 fighter jets and commercial planes cannot communicate with each other. F-15s operate their radios on a UHF frequency while commercial aircraft operate on VHF. It seems no one thought that this could become a problem until the first couple of near-tragedies took place.

Focusing almost exclusively on countermeasures ensures that the system will create nearly as many vulnerabilities as are eliminated. Remember Reality #6: *Aviation security policies often do things we didn't expect them to do.* Real security is a process, not merely a series of countermeasures launched against perceived threats. Conceptualizing aviation security as merely an arena for countermeasures sets up the system to be compromised in the future.

On the other hand, managing risk is an ongoing and continuous process. We can accept the risk, reduce it, or work with some combination of the two. The options available are much greater in number and effectiveness. A security system that is founded upon managing risk doesn't require perfection. It only needs to be able to fail securely and safely. In the end, such a system succeeds based upon human prevention, detection, and response to threats. Countermeasures and technologies provide tactics that are used to accomplish higher security standards. They are tools in a dynamic approach to managing risk that is centered around human intelligence and analysis.

# CONDUCTING RISK ANALYSIS

Risk analysis is a process to ensure that the security controls for a system are fully commensurate with its risks. There is no such thing as 100 percent security. There will always remain risks to the system. Conduct of risk analysis is centered on three main activities:

- ✈ Identifying potential threats
- ✈ Determining existing and possible vulnerabilities
- ✈ Discerning measures, as necessary, that lead to risk reduction

## Identifying Potential Threats

Threat identification is the first step in the risk analysis process. If threats are not accurately identified, the risks they represent cannot be managed or eliminated. In identifying the potential threats, the system needs to determine clearly who desires to inflict damage upon it. Moreover, those in the system need to understand the methods these potential perpetrators use to inflict pain or injury. When it comes to aviation, three groups have historically perpetrated violence on the system: terrorists, criminals, and, more recently, disruptive passengers. Their methods have included aircraft sabotage, in-flight assault, hijacking, airport sabotage, and airport assault. Chapter 8 will fully explore the matrix of the threats against aviation.

## Determining Existing and Possible Vulnerabilities

Vulnerabilities are those elements that make a system more prone to attack by a threat or allow an attack to have a higher degree of success or impact. Vulnerabilities are weaknesses that can be exploited by blows to the system. Chapter 9 will take a look at the vulnerabilities that currently exist within the aviation security system.

## Discerning Measures That Can Lead to Risk Reduction

Measures are actions that can work toward reducing or eliminating the causes or reducing the effects of one or more vulnerabilities. Measures are identified and integrated into a scenario, and the risk rating for that scenario is recalculated to account for the effect of it. Measures can be prioritized by considering a number of factors, including:

- What security problems does the measure solve?
- How well does the measure solve the security problem?
- What other problems might the measure cause?
- What are the costs of the measure?
- Do the costs of the control justify its implementation?[2]

The ultimate objective of this undertaking is to open up debate and discussion about aviation security, and look at it with a completely new set of eyes. The old ways have failed us. If we continue to use them, we will be doomed to the same mistakes as in the past. Let us look further.

# CHAPTER 8
# AVIATION AND VIOLENCE

"A terrorist only has to succeed once, we can never fail."

—Margaret Thatcher

Violence or the threat of violence against aviation traces itself back almost to the origins of commercial flight. The first known case of commercial aviation violence occurred in the skies over Chesterton, Indiana, on October 10, 1933. A United Airlines transcontinental flight bound for Oakland left Newark at 4:30 P.M. and stopped in Cleveland to change pilots. At 6:57 P.M. the Boeing 247, with four passengers and three flight crew aboard, left Cleveland for Chicago and passed over Toledo some forty-three minutes later. At 8:45 P.M., the pilot, Richard Tarrant of Oak Park, Illinois, radioed from over North Liberty, Indiana, that all was well and he was flying at an altitude of fifteen hundred feet.

A little after 9:00 P.M., several residents of this small northwest Indiana town reported hearing and seeing an explosion in the sky. John Tillotson, who lived near to where the plane went down, said he was sitting by a window when the plane exploded and he saw it clearly. He believed that he heard screams and a woman's voice shouting, "Help! Help! Oh my God."[1] According to other witnesses who also observed the first explosion, the plane blew up a second time upon hitting the ground. All on board perished, including the first flight attendant to be killed while on duty, Alice Scribner, 26, of Chicago.

It was believed the plane was flying west on scheduled time and in apparently fine condition. Given the nature of the wreckage, the size of the debris field of the crash, and the testimony of dozens of witnesses, conclusions for the reasons of the crash immediately focused on a bomb. Eventually the U.S. Department of Commerce aeronautics branch concluded the aircraft was destroyed by an explosive device placed in the cargo hold, possibly a container of nitroglycerin attached to a timing device. Although no suspects were ever charged in the bombing, it was more likely a criminal attack than a politically motivated one.[2]

Aviation provides a tremendous amount of opportunity to individuals or groups seeking to achieve their violent ends. First criminals and later terrorists realized that aviation gave them access to a wide variety of options when it came to getting what they wanted. Criminals have traditionally looked upon aviation as an environment ripe with offerings. Billions of tons of cargo, hundreds of millions of passengers, and the ability to move easily and, more recently, affordably between long distances has lured criminals to use aviation as one of the most viable means to wreak havoc. For terrorists, aviation has long served as a target-rich environment and international stage to trumpet their political, social, or religious beliefs. Moreover, we have seen that air travel provides disruptive passengers a venue to exhibit a wide variety of aberrant, abnormal, or abusive behaviors.

Criminal activities against aviation range from the petty, as in the case of the theft of a pocketbook or wallet from a passenger inside an airport terminal, to the marginal, as when a drunken passenger threatens a gate agent, to the catastrophic, as what unfolded on September 11, 2001. Consequently, it is the highest goal of aviation security to lessen the amount of violence perpetrated against the aviation system.

To truly appreciate the ultimate mission of aviation security, it is first necessary to understand the perpetrators of violence against it and the ways in which they succeed. By focusing on the most violent individuals and groups, security personnel can better look at the inherent vulnerabilities within the existing system and think about how to best manage the risks those vulnerabilities present. Finally, based on those analyses they can develop security policies and measures that are proactive enough to anticipate potential threats.

We need to look first at the ways that violence enters into the aviation system. There are essentially five categories of violence against aviation—aircraft sabotage, in-flight assault, hijacking, airport sabotage, and airport assault—that are used by three categories of perpetrators—criminals, terrorists, and disruptive passengers. The following table shows the primary perpetrators of violence against aviation and their preferred methods.

### Primary Perpetrators of Aviation Violence and Their Preferred Methods

|  | Aircraft Sabotage | In-flight Assault | Hijacking | Airport Sabotage | Airport Assault |
|---|---|---|---|---|---|
| Terrorists | X | X | X | X | X |
| Criminals | X |  | X | X | X |
| Disruptive Passengers |  | X | X |  | X |

Before detailing each of the perpetrators and their preferred methods of violence, it is important to note that a fourth group that has committed and is prone in the future to commit violence against aviation was intentionally left out: flight crews. In the estimated 100 million-plus commercial airline flights that have taken place since 1980, there have been less than a dozen documented cases where investigators concluded that deliberate action on the part of a crew member caused a major aircraft accident.[3] The resultant deaths of passengers and crews in all these flight-crew-sabotaged flights is probably in the low thousands. Although this is a significant number, we'll soon see that realistically trying to do something to prevent such actions is nearly impossible.

On December 19, 1997, a SilkAir 737 crashed near Palembang, Indonesia, killing all 104 passengers and crew. The plane, almost brand new, cruising in good weather with an experienced crew, suddenly dropped from a normal flight altitude of thirty-five thousand feet and crashed at a high speed into the Sumatran jungle. The right wing and parts of the rudder separated from the aircraft before it crashed. The Indonesian National Transportation Committee found insufficient evidence to find a cause for the accident. The U.S. National Transportation Safety Board strongly disagreed, finding that the jet's cockpit voice recorder was intentionally disconnected and its flight controls placed in a nose-down position—most likely by the captain. On August 21, 1994, a Morrocan Royal Air Maroc ATR-42-300 with forty-four passengers and crew aboard entered a steep dive from sixteen thousand feet and crashed ten minutes after taking off from Agadir on the Atlantic coast. The pilot was blamed for disconnecting the autopilot and deliberately causing the crash and committing suicide.

These and other suspected crashes involving flight-crew sabotage were almost impossible to prevent, unlike the violent actions of terrorists, criminals, and disruptive passengers. For aviation security planners to try to anticipate such incidents would be a waste of valuable time and precious resources. Therefore, flight crews will not be included within the remainder of the discussion here.

# TERRORISTS

Generally speaking, terrorists are zealots or pawns who believe they are participants in a dynamic social or political process. These people or groups believe that they cannot achieve the changes they desire through the normal political process, so they use violence. In doing so, they have no compunction about killing innocent civilians—be they babies, children, women, or men. Most acts of terrorism are committed to gain publicity for an organization and its purpose, to achieve political goals, or to warrant a response from the entity that is being attacked. By performing sensational acts that attract media attention and outrage from the public, terrorists most often seek a government reaction that will further their cause.

Terrorist operations, including those against aviation, are generally planned over long periods of time and carried out with relatively high levels of expertise. Terrorists seek to exploit the target's vulnerabilities and, with the exception of suicide attackers, minimize their own risk. All forms of terrorist action are, in their most basic form, simple criminal acts. The manner in which they are carried out, the victims that are targeted, and the desired media attention and outcomes are actually the only differences between terrorists and common criminals.

Since 9/11, suicide bombers have moved to the forefront of discussions surrounding aviation security policy. Prior to 9/11 suicide bombers were often portrayed as lone mad zealots, but they are just as likely to be pawns in large terrorist networks that wage calculated psychological warfare. Most terrorists, while willing to risk their lives, do not undertake actions that require their deaths in order to succeed. They wish to live after the terrorist act in order to benefit from their accomplishments.

The motivations of suicide terrorists are different, however. They never perceive their deaths as suicides; rather, they see them as acts of martyrdom. The leaders of terrorist networks are cold and rational, rather than suicidal. For them, suicide terrorism has the following inherent tactical advantages over "conventional" terrorism:[4]

✈ It is a simple and low-cost operation (requiring no escape routes or complicated rescue operations).

✈ It guarantees massive casualties and extensive damage (since the suicide bomber can choose the exact time, location, and circumstances of the attack).

✈ There is no fear that interrogated terrorists will surrender important information (because their deaths are certain).

✈ It has an immense impact on the public and the media (due to the overwhelming sense of helplessness).

✈ The only real disadvantage is that you you need to find and train new recruits, but in some countries, there are plenty of them to be had.

Over most of the twentieth century, terrorists tended to desire attention first and then a large body count. Despite providing extensive television coverage, hijackings—the preferred method for aviation terrorists throughout most of the past decades—often failed to reach far beyond the event itself. This was primarily the case because terrorists are first and foremost driven by a fanatical obsession with immediate success rather than far-reaching effect. That is, they tend to have an arguably higher drive to achieve success than almost any other type of organization or group.[5] Simply put, the terrorists' action has to succeed if anybody is to be terrorized. For this same reason, terrorists traditionally adhere to the same narrow, tried-and-true repertoire of tactics. The result is that the vast majority of the terrorist attacks are tactically not very innovative.[6] The September 11 attacks fell within this parameter. The plan used well-proven tactics—hijackings and suicide pilots—to deliver their weapons to predetermined targets. The attacks, at their core, used hijacked airliners (the delivery system) to deliver jet fuel (the weapon of mass destruction) to predetermined ground targets to wreak severe damage and kill the people on board.

# CRIMINALS

There is no proven scientific explanation as to why certain people commit certain crimes. Criminology, which includes the study of why people commit crime, tends to focus on two main types of theories—microtheories and macrotherories—to answer this question. *Microtheories* primarily look at the individual. They explore why individuals become criminals and what might be wrong with the individuals that makes them criminals. *Macrotheories*, on the other hand, focus upon how the social structure affects criminal behavior. They seek to know what it is in society that drives people to criminal activity and generally look at criminal behavior in groups of people rather than in individuals. Whatever the explanation for what makes criminals do what they do, it is clear that aviation has always attracted criminals to achieve their ends.

## A Subset of Terrorists and Criminals: Corrupt Insiders

Another group that is not specifically included within the scheme of perpetrators of violence against aviation, but who play an active role, are corrupt insiders. They tend to fall within the criminal category. However, they can also be well-placed terrorists who offer assistance to outside members of their organization when the time to strike is at hand. The methods of violence they use are the same as criminals and terrorists. Attacks by insiders are not anything new, especially since they typically know their way around the inner workings of the security system and how to circumvent it better than almost anyone else. Personal revenge, a desire to enrich themselves, or any other number of reasons can motivate corrupt insiders.

## DISRUPTIVE PASSENGERS

Disruptive passengers are often overlooked when trying to recognize the role violence plays within the aviation system. Although terrorist acts against aviation receive much more attention from both policy planners and the media, disruptive passengers pose a much more pervasive, ongoing threat. The sheer number of cases that take place every year evidences this.

Despite heightened awareness and new security measures, the number of disruptive passenger incidents totaled more than eight thousand at the nation's twenty-five busiest airports during the period of September 1, 2001, to December 31, 2001, alone (see table 4). A disruptive passenger incident was defined as "aberrant, abnormal, or abusive behavior on the part of passengers either at airports or onboard commercial flights."[7] The data were gleaned using analyses of FAA records, FBI records, local law enforcement records, and airline incident reports as well as interviews with FAA civil aviation specialists, FAA flight standards employees, FBI agents, local law enforcement personnel, flight crews, airport security personnel, and airline security personnel.

Yet despite the plethora of new aviation security measures currently put in place, the critical issue of disruptive passengers has barely hit the radar screen. This is unfortunate, given the number of out-of-control passengers witnessed both before and after the September 11 terrorist attacks. In the twenty-four months leading up to September 11, 2001, there were thirty documented cockpit intrusions by disruptive passengers on commercial carriers. The actions of disruptive passengers and the total lack of response by authorities to deal with the problem instructed the 9/11 terrorists on the ease with which they could enter the cockpit. This education continues.

On August 20, 2002, an Air France flight bound for Oslo, Norway, was forced to make an emergency landing in Belgium after a naked passenger tried to storm the cockpit. The flight,

## Table 4. Disruptive Passenger Incidents
## at the Nation's 25 Busiest Airports

## September 1, 2001–December 31, 2001

| Airport Ranking | Airport | # of Disruptive Incidents | Passenger Volume Ranking |
|---|---|---|---|
| 1 | Atlanta (ATL) | 546 | 1 |
| 2 | Los Angeles (LAX) | 531 | 4 |
| 3 | San Francisco (SFO) | 494 | 5 |
| 4 | Las Vegas (LAS) | 474 | 7 |
| 5 | Chicago O'Hare (ORD) | 465 | 2 |
| 6 | Dallas/Fort Worth (DFW) | 433 | 3 |
| 7 | Dulles (IAD) | 432 | 22 |
| 8 | Miami (MIA) | 428 | 13 |
| 9 | New York Kennedy (JFK) | 402 | 14 |
| 10 | Boston (BOS) | 402 | 18 |
| 11 | Detroit (DTW) | 396 | 10 |
| 12 | Phildelphia (PHL) | 375 | 20 |
| 13 | New York La Guardia (LGA) | 367 | 19 |
| 14 | Newark (EWR) | 347 | 12 |
| 15 | Houston (IAH) | 337 | 11 |
| 16 | St. Louis (STL) | 251 | 16 |
| 17 | Seattle (SEA) | 245 | 17 |
| 18 | Phoenix (PHX) | 235 | 9 |
| 19 | Denver (DIA) | 229 | 6 |
| 20 | Orlando (MCO) | 193 | 15 |
| 21 | Salt Lake City (SLC) | 168 | 23 |
| 22 | Charlotte (CLT) | 147 | 21 |
| 23 | San Diego (SAN) | 138 | 25 |
| 24 | Minneapolis (MSP) | 117 | 8 |
| 25 | Memphis (MEM) | 112 | 24 |
| | **TOTAL** | **8,264** | |

which left Paris, was rerouted to Brussels International Airport after the thirty-one-year-old stripped off all his clothes at his seat and tried to force his way into the cockpit. The pilot of the plane requested help from Belgian air traffic control that allowed the plane to land. The man, a French national of Tunisian origin was removed from the plane and arrested by police. He was later released without being charged.

On July 10, 2002, police arrested a thirty-five-year-old British man for trying to enter the cockpit of a flight from Cape Town, South Africa, to London. It appeared that he attempted to enter the cockpit while the aircraft was in flight. About six hours into the flight, the man got up from his seat, walked to the plane's upper deck, ran down the aisle and rammed his shoulder into the locked cockpit door. He repeatedly hit the door, trying to break in. Other passengers and crewmembers quickly overpowered and handcuffed the man, and a doctor onboard examined him, reporting that the man had suffered a panic attack after taking some prescribed medicine.

On February 7, 2002, United Airlines flight 855 took off from Miami at midnight with 142 passengers and 15 crewmembers aboard. About five hours into the flight, as the jetliner flew over Brazil, a twenty-eight-year-old Uruguayan passenger began kicking the cockpit door of the Boeing 777. He kicked in a small breakaway panel across the bottom half of the door and then stuck his head inside the cockpit. At that point, one of the pilots grabbed a small ax and hit him in the head, subduing him.

## AIRCRAFT SABOTAGE

Violent acts of sabotage against an aircraft include shoot-ats, cargo theft, aircraft bombing, and commandeering.

### Shoot-Ats

"Shoot-ats" are incidents in which in-flight aircraft (commercial and general/charter aviation) are fired upon either from the ground (surface-to-air missiles [SAMs], antiaircraft artillery, small arms fire, etc.) or from the air. In April 1994, the presidents of

Rwanda and Burundi were killed aboard the Rwandan presidential jet (a Falcon 50 registered 9xR-NN) when a SAM hit it while the plane was on final approach to the international airport at Kigali, Rwanda, thus sparking Rwanda's Hutu-Tutsi civil war. In September 1993, Abkhazian separatists of the ex-Soviet republic of Georgia shot down—or blew up on the runway— three Tu-134 and Tu-154 airliners using shoulder-fired SAMs from boats out on the Black Sea. These attacks were notable as the first to be launched from boats. In 1986, a Sudan Airways jet was shot down by a SAM, and in the late 1970s, two Rhodesian (now Zimbabwean) airliners were reportedly shot down by SA-7s.

More recently, the long history of shoot-ats reared its ugly head again when an Israeli charter jet was shot at by two SAMs while over Mombasa, Kenya, in November 2002. The SA-7 missiles were reportedly the same kind that Al Qaeda transported out of Afghanistan in late 2001. After U.S. intervention in October 2001, Al Qaeda moved a number of SAMs into the Arabian peninusla and to the Horn of Africa. In May of 2002 an Al Qaeda member from the Sudan fired an SA-7 at a U.S. military aircraft in the vicinity of the Prince Sudan Air Base in Saudi Arabia.

## Cargo Theft

Theft of cargo from airplanes is a worldwide problem for aviation security personnel. Cargo theft takes various forms, from baggage handlers stealing from passengers' luggage to armed assaults targeting specific cargo, such as money or jewelry. Perpetrators intent on cargo theft generally use one of two modus operandi in carrying out an armed assault: (1) perpetrators may carry out an airport invasion: enter the air operations area by force and steal cargo from the aircraft while the plane is still on the ground; (2) they may board the plane, hijack the flight, and force the crew to land at a predetermined location where the cargo may be off-loaded.

In most incidents, the thieves have foreknowledge of the specific flight, its cargo, and the ways to circumvent security. This suggests either insider knowledge or thorough surveillance of the target. Airport invasions may outnumber hijackings or the commandeering of aircrafts to another location because of the greater risks and difficulties involved in the latter, including the logistics of getting an aircraft to land at a predetermined location where co-conspirators are waiting. Another reason thieves avoid hijacking, at least at more secure airports, is effective preboard security measures, which present a formidable barrier to successfully boarding an aircraft while armed.

### Cargo Theft: A Criminal Case Study

In the late 1990s, cargo theft at New York's JFK became a particular concern for those in air cargo security because of the large volume of air freight handled there each year. In 2000, approximately 1.8 million tons of air cargo valued at approximately $120 billion was shipped through JFK International Airport. This constituted the fourth largest amount in the nation and fifth in the world (behind Tokyo, Memphis, Miami, and Los Angeles).

To combat the heists, Operation Kat-Net (Kennedy Airport Theft Network) was authorized in 1996 by the district attorney's office, which eventually resulted in the arrest of more than eighty individuals involved in thefts from air cargo facilities located at and around JFK airport. The arrests were the culmination of a three-year investigation that recovered in excess of $14 million worth of stolen goods. This investigation was conducted jointly by the FBI, the United States Attorney's Office for the Eastern District of New York, the NY/NJ Port Authority, and the New York State Police. It employed the use of undercover agents and the execution of federal and state court-authorized eavesdropping warrants. The sting operation was based in a warehouse near JFK and equipped agents with the ability to recover millions of dollars worth of stolen property. The property that was stolen and recovered included avionics parts, designer clothing, luxury automobiles, jewelry, perfumes, firearms, computer equipment, camcorders, and cellular telephones.[8]

## Aircraft Bombing

The bombing of aircraft has long been a preferred technique for both terrorists and criminals. For terrorists, commercial airliners in particular have afforded a wonderful opportunity to grab the attention they covet so much. Airliners in much of the world are viewed as symbols of the nation whose flag is painted on the rear tail. Attacking a nation's commercial air carrier is metaphorically waging battle against the nation itself. For "ordinary" criminals, blowing up an aircraft opens the door for them to capitalize on insurance claims or to take down rivals.

### Aircraft Bombing: A Terrorist Case Study

On December 22, 2001, American Airlines flight 63 from Paris to Miami made an emergency landing in Boston after a passenger tried to blow up his sneakers. Richard Reid, a British-born twenty-eight-year-old, was seen trying to light the inner tongue of his sneaker, from which a wire was protruding. He was subdued by flight attendants and passengers who pinned him down. In the struggle, he bit a flight attendant. Two French doctors on board the flight injected three drugs into Reid, including an antihistamine and the sedatives Valium and Narcan, in an effort to subdue him. The plane was diverted to Boston where Reid was taken into custody.

During a court appearance in 2002 in which Reid surprisingly changed his plea to guilty, he was asked by the presiding judge if he agreed with the government's description of what happened on the flight. "Basically, I got on the plane with a bomb. Basically, I tried to ignite it. Basically, yeah, intended to damage the plane,"

Reid said laughing, adding later that he was a disciple of Osama bin Laden and an enemy of the United States.[9]

*Aircraft Bombing: A Criminal Case Study*

On November 1, 1955, at 6:52 P.M. United Airlines flight 629, a DC-6B with forty-four people aboard, took off from Stapleton Airport in Denver, bound for Seattle. Eleven minutes later, the thirty-nine passengers, including an infant, and five crew members were dead—killed instantly when the airliner exploded above a sugar beet farm near Longmont, Colorado.

An examination of fragments and pieces of wreckage recovered from the crash and examined by an FBI laboratory, revealed foreign deposits ranging in color from white to very dark gray. These deposits consisted mainly of sodium carbonate, although nitrate and sulfur compounds were present as well. Laboratory technicians informed their colleagues that at the time dynamite consisted of nitroglycerin with varying amounts of sodium carbonate, sodium nitrate, and sulfur-bearing compounds.

As the investigation progressed, background data on each of the forty-four victims were investigated. Motives for homicide against any of the victims were explored. Immediate efforts were undertaken to identify those passengers who had large amounts of insurance coverage. In the following days, it was discovered that one passenger, Daisie E. King, had three life insurance policies in her name. One was a travel insurance policy in the amount of $37,500. Two other policies, each for $6,250, also were taken out on the life of King. Further analysis by the FBI revealed that upon her death, King's son, Jack Gilbert Graham, was to receive a substantial inheritance in addition to the life insurance policies.

After several interrogations by FBI investigators, Graham finally admitted he had constructed a time bomb and placed it in his mother's luggage. He said wanted to cause his mother's death so that he could cash in on her substantial life- and travel-insurance policies. Graham said the device consisted of twenty-five sticks of dynamite, two electric primer caps, a timer, and a six-volt battery. He went on to admit that after he had assembled the bomb, he slipped the weapon into his mother's old battered luggage, and fastened the suitcase with some extra tape for security. After Graham dropped off his mother at the terminal door, he drove to an airport parking lot. There, he unloaded his mother's suitcase from the car and set the timer to the bomb. He next took the suitcase to the counter for weighing before it was to be placed on the aircraft. For the premeditated murder of his mother, Jack Gilbert Graham was sentenced to death and was executed in Colorado's gas chamber on January 11, 1957.[10]

*Aircraft Bombing: A Terrorist Case Study*

French prosecutors believe terrorists wanted to blow up a Moroccan passenger aircraft after explosives similar to the ones used by Richard Reid were discovered on a Royal Air Maroc airplane, after it landed in eastern France on September 25, 2002. There was no detonator attached to the three and a half ounces of explosives, which were found in the passenger section of the plane during a search by customs agents. The plane took off from the French port city of Marseilles for the Moroccan capital of Marrakesh before heading to the Metz-Lorraine-Nancy airport in eastern France. It remains unclear how or when the explosives were brought onboard. The material was identified as pentrite—the same substance Reid had tried to detonate on an American Airlines flight from Paris to Miami less than a year earlier.

## Commandeering

Commandeerings occur when the aircraft is on the ground and the doors are open. Commandeering refers to seizing or taking over an aircraft without authority. Although all types of aircraft can and are commandeered, general or charter aircraft tend to be taken over more often than commercial airliners. The security at general aviation airports is typically much less stringent than at commercial ones. Airport perimeters are more porous and security regimens much less intense.

### Commandeering: A Terrorist Case Study

On January 5, 2002, fifteen-year-old Charles J. Bishop commandeered a small Cessna airplane and deliberately crashed it into a Tampa office building. In what authorities came to believe was a suicide note, Bishop indicated his support for Osama bin Laden and that the act was deliberate. Bishop, who took the plane on an unauthorized flight across Tampa Bay, died as he crashed into the forty-two-story Bank of America Plaza building. "I would characterize it as a suicide," said Tampa Police Chief Bennie Holder. The note, which was found in the wreckage of the plane, "clearly stated that he had acted alone, without any help from anyone else," Holder said. "He did, however, make statements expressing his sympathy for Osama bin Laden and the events which occurred September 11, 2001."

Bishop, who had taken flight lessons for two years, had gone to the private-plane section of the St. Petersburg–Clearwater International Airport, accompanied by his mother and grandmother. His instructor left him at the plane to perform a preflight inspection, authorities said. He had no authority to get in the plane alone, a government transportation official said. A ninth-grader at East Lake High School near Tarpon Springs, Florida, Bishop should have had an instructor in the plane with him, said Pinellas County Sheriff's Department spokesman Sgt. Greg Tita. Once he was alone in the plane, a Cessna 172, he started the engine and took off without permission around 5 P.M. EST. When the plane took off, the instructor contacted the St. Petersburg airport's air-traffic control tower, which then notified Tampa International Airport, Tampa police said. The St. Petersburg control tower also immediately notified MacDill Air Force Base since the Cessna was headed its way, said Sgt. Chris Miller, MacDill public affairs officer. After a five-minute flight over Tampa Bay, the plane entered MacDill Air Force Base's restricted airspace and flew over the runway about one hundred feet off the ground, Miller said. The student did not appear to be making an attempt to land nor did the plane circle or fly erratically, he added. The helicopter caught up with the plane near Peter O. Knight Airport, about fourteen miles east from where the Cessna took off, said Coast Guard spokesman Paul Rhymand.

Minutes before the crash, the helicopter pilot made direct eye contact with the student through the chopper's open side door as crew members gestured for Bishop to land the plane, police said. It was not clear what his response was. Beyond making gestures, "There's not much a helicopter can do," said Coast Guard spokeswoman Lt. Charlotte Pittman. She was sure that the youth saw the crew's hand gestures, Pittman said. Soon after, the plane crashed into the Bank of America building. The plane's wings fell to the ground, but the fuselage stuck in the building's southwest corner on the twenty-eighth and twenty-ninth floors. Bishop was killed.[11]

## IN-FLIGHT ASSAULT

The vast majority of violent in-flight assaults are committed by disruptive passengers. These actions are taken against either other passengers or flight crews. In recent years, aberrant, abusive, or abnormal behavior by disruptive passengers in airports and on commercial airlines has become increasingly common. This behavior—popularly known as air rage—remains the most pervasive threat to the safety and security of the 1.5 billion passengers who travel by air each year.

The rise in the scope and intensity of air rage incidents can be attributed to a number of factors, including alcohol consumption before and during flights; the taking of illegal narcotics; the inability of passengers to smoke on most aircraft and within most airports; mounting distrust of fellow passengers; growing frustration with new security measures and the delays they cause; the effects of mental illness on some passengers; and, the continued policy of deporting illegal aliens on commercial airliners unescorted and unrestrained.

## Alcohol Abuse: A Disruptive Passenger Case Study

In August 2002, Briton Victor Mardell was flying on an Air 2000 flight from Manchester, England, to Orlando, Florida, to surprise his relatives at his son's wedding at Cypress Gardens, even though he wasn't invited to the ceremony. About three hours after takeoff, flight attendants twice had to confiscate bottles of Jameson whiskey from Mardell. Allegedly, the disruptive passenger tried to open the plane's door while in flight, was verbally abusive to a boy sitting next to him, pushed a flight attendant against a bathroom door, and twice had to be restrained by other passengers.[12] Mardell was arrested at Orlando's Sanford Airport.

## Distrust of Fellow Travelers:
## A Disruptive Passenger Case Study

A Spirit Airlines flight from Orlando to New York on September 26, 2002, was forced to return to Orlando International Airport (OIA) after passengers began screaming at two fellow travelers who looked suspicious, authorities said. The unidentified passengers, who were predominantly Orthodox Jews, became unruly after apparently singling out two young men who appeared to be Middle Eastern. The pair was later determined to be of Guyanese descent. Flight 1864, with 137 passengers, left OIA at 3:30 P.M. After the fracas, the crew made a U-turn three miles south of Jacksonville. By 4 P.M., the MD-80 was back at OIA.[13]

## Frustration with Security Measures:
## A Disruptive Passenger Case Study

On September 24, 2002, a California county sheriff was ordered off a United Express flight because he was being a belligerent and frightening passenger, an airline spokeswoman said. The Siskiyou County Sheriff "said some very profane things" when a security guard told him he had been randomly selected for further security checks, said Sabrena Suite, spokeswoman for SkyWest Airlines, which operates some United Express flights on the West Coast. The sheriff said that the incident during boarding for the Redding–to–San Francisco flight was prompted by "some type of misunderstanding on the part of airport personnel." The veteran sheriff was seeking reelection to his fifth term in November.[14]

## Illegal Deportees: A Disruptive Passenger Case Study

On August 29, 2002, an illegal alien from Albania who was being deported tried to strangle a flight attendant with his shoelaces. The incident occurred aboard a Montenegro Airlines flight from Düsseldorf, Germany, to Pristina, Kosovo. The illegal got up to go to the toilet, where he took the laces out of his running shoes. He then came up from behind flight attendant Irena Radonjic and tried to strangle her. Passengers and other flight crew reacted immediately and subdued the attacker. Later, when asked about the incident, an airline spokesperson said, "'We don't really know what was in the attacker's head. When the flight attendant was serving refreshments and asked him what he would like to drink he replied, "A little blood from you."[15]

Dishearteningly, the vast majority of in-flight cases are never reported to the proper authorities. At most airports, local law enforcement is the only entity to receive the call when a disruptive passenger acts out. If a local police report is not filed immediately, the case often disappears. The TSA and FBI are never even notified of the incident.

# HIJACKING

An incident is defined as a hijacking rather than a commandeering when the aircraft has in-flight status. That is, once the doors are closed. By this definition, a hijacking can occur on the ground. The motives for hijackings vary widely. All three categories of perpetrators—terrorists, criminals, and disruptive passengers—who commit violence against aviation use hijacking as a tool.

Before September 11, 2001, an aircraft hijacking usually meant the takeover of an aircraft by an armed group intending to use passengers as hostages to advance its interests. Hijackings "normally" followed a pattern of negotiations between the hijackers and the authorities, followed by some form of settlement (not always the meeting of the hijackers' demands), or the storming of the aircraft by armed police or special forces to rescue the hostages.

The first recorded aircraft hijack was on February 21, 1931, in Arequipa, Peru. Byron Rickards, flying a Ford Tri-motor, was approached on the ground by armed revolutionaries. He refused to fly them anywhere, and after a ten-day stand-off Rickards was informed that the revolution was successful. He would be let go in return for giving one of the revolutionaries a lift to Lima. However, most hijackings have not been so farcical. The first hijack of an airliner probably happened on July 16, 1948, when a failed attempt to gain control of a Cathay Pacific airliner caused it to crash into the sea off Macao, China.

Since 1947, approximately 60 percent of hijackings have been refugee escapes. From the beginning, most hijacking incidents involved individuals or groups of individuals trying to get away from political or economic conditions in their homeland, such as Cuba. Terrorists discovered the benefits of hijackings as a viable tactic in the late 1960s, and leveraged the option to its fullest, culminating with the September 11, 2001, attacks. Criminals tend to use hijacking only as a last resort to accomplish their goals. Hijacking can be very complicated with too many variables, which flies in the face of the kinds of simple methods criminals prefer. Disruptive passenger incidents can escalate into hijackings as distraught, drunk, or deranged passengers look for other ways to act out their intentions.

### Hijacking: A Disruptive Passenger Case Study

A Colombian airliner made an emergency landing at a Spanish military base on July 19, 2002, after a passenger threatened to hijack the plane. Avianca flight 10 was flying from Bogotá, Colombia, to Madrid's Barajas Airport with 144 passengers and 11 crewmembers when a passenger allegedly brandished a plastic knife. Juan Carlos Velez, director of Colombian Civil Aviation, said the passenger also used a pen and a cigarette lighter in making his threats. He was subdued by passengers and flight crew. An F-18 fighter jet accompanied the plane during its diversion to the Torrejon, Spain, air base, where the suspect was taken into custody. A spokeswoman for the Colombian Embassy said the passenger and a companion reportedly were drinking alcohol before the flight left Bogotá. Spokeswoman Lina Munera said, "It really seems a case more related to alcohol than a hijacking."[16]

## AIRPORT SABOTAGE

Airport sabotage includes bombings and attempted bombings of aviation facilities, shootings, shellings (mortar attacks), arsons, and similar incidents. These incidents are primarily the work of terrorists, although criminals will occasionally engage in such actions. Air traffic control facilities are also covered in this category, although in many places around the world they are located outside of the perimeter of the airport.

## Airport Sabotage: A Terrorist Case Study

In Colombo, Sri Lanka, on July 22, 2001, suicide squads from the terrorist group Liberation Tigers of Tamil Eelam struck devastatingly at the capital's airport, damaging a dozen aircraft and killing seven airport personnel. For most of the day, Sri Lankan elite special forces personnel engaged in a relentless battle with the terrorists as the assailants fired at civilian aircraft on the tarmac of the Bandaranaike International Airport, completely destroying half of the fleet of Sri Lankan Airlines. Eventually, thirteen terrorists were killed.

## Airport Sabotage: A Criminal Case Study

An explosive device detonated in a garbage can between the international and domestic departure halls at Cape Town International Airport in South Africa on July 18, 2000. The bomb blast littered the road and a nearby parking lot with debris. It severely damaged two cars. The blast even catapulted a section of the garbage can over the roof of the terminal building and onto the parking apron. Fortunately, no one was injured, partly because a heavy rain kept people inside the terminal at the time of the explosion. No one claimed responsibility for the attack, but it coincided with the appearance in court of two People Against Gangsterism and Drugs (PAGAD) members being tried in connection with urban terrorism. The national director of public prosecutions said that he believed that the bombing was "an attempt by [PAGAD] to show they are still alive, not dead."

# AIRPORT ASSAULT

Airport terminals and concourses are some of the most crowded places on earth. Hartsfield International Airport in Atlanta—the world's busiest airport—handles more than 75 million passengers a year. More than ten thousand workers are employed there, performing every imaginable function from food service to administration to security. Hartsfield handles some twenty-four hundred planes a day.[17] Such places are obviously vulnerable to terrorists, criminals, and disruptive passengers.

## Airport Assault: A Criminal Case Study

On November 13, 1998, an individual approached the main domestic checkpoint at Atlanta's Hartsfield International Airport and placed a loaded .45 caliber handgun at the back of a ticketed passenger. He told the passenger to keep walking and not turn around. When a checkpoint screener challenged the man holding the gun, he doused the back of his hostage with lighter fluid and tried to force his way through. He was immediately apprehended and arrested by police. The handgun was loaded with eight bullets, and the individual had matches and a knife in his pocket. The individual was charged with several offenses, including aggravated assault, terrorist threats, and carrying an incendiary device, and was incarcerated at the Clayton County jail in Jonesboro, Georgia. A motive for the action was never discovered.

## Airport Assault: A Criminal Case Study

On February 17, 1999, an armed robbery occurred on the tarmac at Brussels National Airport. Four thieves stole approximately $1.6 million in money and jewelry from an armored car that was transferring money to a Virgin Express flight to London's Heathrow Airport. The robbery occurred minutes before the plane was to depart and took very little time. Reports indicated that the thieves, disguised as Sabena Airline employees, had forced open a locked gate. They then drove onto the runway, ordered baggage handlers to hand over containers of money, and escaped. The plane's five crew members were onboard but were unaware of the robbery; the plane's thirty-three passengers were in the terminal at the time. All the suspects were eventually caught.

## Airport Assault: A Terrorist Case Study

An attack at the El Al ticket counter in Los Angeles Airport (LAX) on July 4, 2002, revealed that terrorists still view airport assaults as a means to an end. LAX ticket agent Victoria Hen foiled a potential terrorist act when Hesham Mohamed Hadayet, a forty-one-year-old businessman from suburban Irvine, California, pulled a gun in the crowded El Al check-in area. After the gunman shot a bystander—Yaakov Aminov, 46, a jeweler and father of eight who was dropping off a friend—the twenty-five-year-old Hen pulled her own weapon and killed the terrorist with a single shot to the chest. In the exchange of gunfire, Hen was shot as well. The perpetrator was armed with two handguns, a six-inch knife, and extra magazines. A witness said, "It all happened so quickly. This guy pulled a gun as I was helping my friend unload some luggage. There was a noise like thunder. I almost fainted, but then the gunman just fell to the ground."[18] Both Hen and the bystander later died as a result of their wounds.

## Airport Assault: A Criminal Case Study

In late 1998, more than $9 million worth of cocaine was discovered under the seats of two British West Indies Airlines (BWIA) aircraft at Toronto's Pearson International Airport over a two-week period. Immediately after the discoveries, authorities pointed fingers at BWIA's maintenance workers. "It certainly appears to be an inside job," Staff Sgt. Bill Matheson of the Royal Canadian Mounted Police told the *Toronto Sun*. "The drugs were left there for someone here to take off." Matheson said 6.6 kilos of cocaine, worth about $6 million, was found under six different seats of one aircraft. Another 3.3 kilos, worth about $3 million, was found under three seats in another airplane the week before. Customs officials said the drugs were wrapped in flat, plastic packages and taped together. The packages were hidden between the seat cushions and frames of different seats in the cabin.

Customs spokesperson Daniel Smith said, "We believe the drugs were to be removed by someone here. We don't believe a passenger left it there." He said the drugs were seized after Customs officers boarded the craft before maintenance crews.

"This is one way of smuggling I haven't heard of before," Smith reported. "Smugglers are always coming up with new ways." And while they were happy about the seizures, Canadian officers again expressed concern about the security implications. "If they (smugglers) could plant drugs on an aircraft at a major international airport, then they could plant anything else they want."[19]

By recognizing how violence is committed against the aviation industry, it becomes easier to establish a viable security system to meet the threats.

# CHAPTER 9

# VULNERABILITIES OF THE AVIATION SECURITY SYSTEM

"The important thing is not to stop questioning."

—Albert Einstein

The dictionary defines the word "vulnerable" as being suscep-tible to physical or emotional injury or attack (as Alexander Hamilton observed about the U.S. military after the Revolutionary War: "We are vulnerable both by water and land, without either fleet or army."); open to censure or criticism; assailable. The first definition is the one that applies most appropriately to aviation security. In its simplest form, a vulnerability is a flaw in the secu-rity of a system that an attacker can exploit to commit damage or injury. Unfortunately, as with many technical issues, the dictionary definition can only help so much. The issue is much more complex. Vulnerabilities cannot always be defined in a clear, cut-and-dry manner. Since they interact with complex systems, and aviation security is a very complex system, what may be a vulnerability in one situation may not be a vulnerability in another.

To get a better sense of what a vulnerability may be, we should start with the broadest possible definition. That is, any access to the system is a potential vulnerability. This leaves those in aviation security with the Herculean task of trying to manage risk proactively for a system that is very accessible. It is only when there is no access that there are no vulnerabilities. But that's an impossibility.

Thus, we do the next best thing: we implement measures that reduce the risk caused by the accessibility to the system. We can't avoid the fact that attackers will always find some degree of access to airplanes and airports. It is an inherent reality in running an airport. We can, however, control to a great extent the amount of access and the areas of access available to the potential attacker.

A vulnerability can also stem from Reality #6 on page 133: *Aviation security measures often do things we didn't expect them to do.* Unintended consequences of measures and countermeasures are a potential vulnerability. When people design a measure, they want it to do certain things. Nonetheless, by implementing and putting a measure into action, it tends to become more complex than it was merely as an idea or a plan on the drawing board. This is exacerbated by the complexity of the aviation system. To be able to plan for all of the contingencies, glitches, and unanticipated problems that invariably arise in a complex system is almost impossible. These types of challenges are what confront those who deal with aviation security problems. Unforeseen problems that may not be very obvious at the outset may arise. In some cases, a long period of time may pass until anyone discovers the unintended vulnerability that a measure has created.

There are currently policies in place that allow air marshals, armed pilots, and law enforcement officers to carry firearms on an aircraft. Although the weapons must stay under the control of a trained professional at all times, the mere presence of a firearm in an aircraft cabin can become a vulnerability if an unforeseen human factor enters into the picture.

As has happened in the past on numerous occasions, a law enforcement officer has used the lavatory and removed his firearm. Upon exiting the lavatory, the officer accidentally leaves the weapon behind. In this scenario, firearms in the air cabin may be regarded as a vulnerability according to this usage of the word. However, a narrower view of the term holds that such an unforeseen result may fall short of being a true vulnerability. It may be argued that although there exists the possibility of a firearm being left in the lavatory by a trained professional onboard an aircraft, the probability of such occurrence helping terrorists, criminals, or disruptive passengers carry out their aims is quite low. The chance of a potential perpetrator coming across a misplaced firearm is minuscule. Therefore, in this case, a firearm on the aircraft mistakenly falling into the hands of an attacker might not be considered a high risk to the aviation security system.

On the other hand, could a team of terrorists intentionally cause a disruption on an aircraft to draw out the two or three air marshals that might be on the flight? Suppose two terrorists rush the cockpit door, trying to force their way in. Although air marshals are trained to work as a team, suppose that each of the marshals on the plane immediately react and draw their weapons on the two cockpit intruders. This would identify the marshals and leave them open to assault from the other three terrorists on the plane who had been lying in wait. Such a situation involving firearms on the aircraft could now make the presence of the weapons a vulnerability that could present a much higher level of risk.

The primary concern of aviation security planners should be exploitable vulnerabilities, like the air marshal scenario. If air marshals are properly trained to remain incognito and possess the self-discipline necessary to do so while their team member is trying to thwart the attack of the first two terrorists, then the level of risk for this exploitable vulnerability would be dramatically decreased. However, if the fellow air marshals lack the knowledge and control to stay seated, then the risk is much higher that a firearm can be seized by terrorists during a flight. This allows a vulnerability to be used to gain unauthorized access to the system or permits the vulnerability to be leveraged to directly attack the system and inflict violence. Unfortunately, such vulnerabilities, which were widely acknowledged as possible problems, have been found in the past. But nothing was ever done to reduce the risk they posed. The cockpit doors on 9/11 provide another example.

A vulnerability can be termed "nonexploitable" if security functions or measures in place prevent exploitation of the vulnerability. If policies are in place that prohibit the cockpit door from ever being opened during a flight, the vulnerability of the cockpit would be pretty much nonexploitable. However, as we've seen, failing to secure the door by allowing it to be opened keeps the cockpit an exploitable vulnerability.

The majority of successful attacks on the aviation system have historically come from capitalizing on only a few exploitable vulnerabilities. This can be attributed to the fact that attackers are opportunistic, take the easiest and most convenient route, and exploit the best-known flaws with the most effective and widely available attack tools. They count on aviation security planners not fixing these problems.

## A SAMPLING OF AVIATION SECURITY VULNERABILITIES

Although tens of thousands of security incidents occur each year affecting aviation, the overwhelming majority of successful attacks fall into a few categories. The following is a random and admittedly incomplete list of vulnerabilities that I believe require some form of immediate action. Several vulnerabilities that are classified or not known outside of the industry have been deliberately left off this list for obvious reasons. It is not the purpose of this book to provide would-be attackers any assistance in causing damage or inflicting violence. Instead, the aim here is to engage the creativity and capabilities of planners to consider a new and better strategic approach to securing the aviation system through risk analysis and assessment.

## Deporting Illegal Aliens on Commercial Flights

Internal reports from the INS suggest that more than thirty-five thousand illegal immigrants were deported from the United States on commercial flights during the year 2002. Of these illegal aliens, more than half have been indicted or involved in criminal activity. Whether waiting in the gate area or approaching the aircraft by vehicle, INS policy requires the deportees to be handcuffed, and, for the more violent types, to be placed also in leg irons. In addition, INS policy mandates that two armed agents be present with the deportee at all times prior to the transfer onto the aircraft. Frighteningly, however, the vast majority of the deportees travel unescorted and unrestrained to their final destination.

INS policy currently states that agents "should" escort groups of ten or more deportees; groups that are fewer than ten travel unescorted (see table 5). According to INS guidelines, internationals with criminal records are allowed to travel unsupervised, as long as they haven't been convicted of violent crimes. In almost every case where there are ten or fewer illegal aliens traveling together, the agents board the aircraft with the deportees prior to the general boarding of the rest of the passengers. The INS agents remain with the deportees until the plane has been completely boarded by other passengers. Then, right before the cabin door is closed, the handcuffs and leg irons are removed and the INS agents get off the plane. So, for the next several hours, the deportees, who just a few minutes earlier were wearing handcuffs and under the supervision of armed guards, are left to wander the cabin like everybody else. This becomes an obvious problem waiting to happen. On a flight from San Diego to El Salvador, two dozen unescorted criminal deportees, just out of jail, stole liquor from a service cart and got drunk. A twelve-year-old girl, traveling

## Table 5. INS Escort Policy for the Deportation of Illegal Aliens

| Group Descriptors | Escort Required |
|---|---|
| **Group 1** | |
| Persons granted or permitted withdrawal of application for admission, or voluntary departure by a Chief Patrol Agent, District Director or an Immigration Judge. This presumes the person has good moral character and no known criminal background or asocial behavior. | No escort required. |
| Persons removed pursuant to an order of removal who have no known criminal background or asocial behavior. | |
| Non-criminal aliens escorted to a point of departure, placed on the carrier and met by other INS officers at the point of arrival. | |
| **Group 1a** | |
| Persons in need of assistance because of age, infirmity, mental capacity, handicap or language barriers. | Minimum of one escort. |
| Medical parolee en route to half-way house or point of release from INS custody. | |
| Unaccompanied juveniles. | One escort of same sex per juvenile. |
| **Group 2** | |
| Persons at any time charged or convicted of non-violent crimes, or known to be criminally involved, determined by an INS officer to be non-violent. | A group of fewer than 10 detainees requires no escorts. Minimum of 2 escorts for a group of 10 detainees. Each additional group of 5 requires 1 more escort. |
| **Group 3** | |
| Persons who are chargeable or were charged or convicted of criminal violations involving threat of force, assault, violence, or killing any person or animal. | At least two escorts per detainee are required. When traveling to destinations within United States, these shall be armed officers. |
| Persons who are or have been verbally abusive, verbally combative, confrontational, vulgar or verbally coercive during the course of their immigration proceedings or custody, or who have otherwise indicated willingness or intent to resist physical removal from the United States pursuant to a lawful order or finding. | |
| Persons who are serving criminal sentences, being transferred or delivered to other jurisdictions where criminal proceedings are pending, regardless of whether or not the crime underlying the unexpired sentence or proceedings involved force or violence. | |
| **Group 3a** | |
| Individuals deemed by the U.S. Public Health Service or by competent medical authority to be in need of medical services during travel. | Minimum of two escorts, plus a medical professional. |

alone to visit relatives and seated amid the criminals, was inappropriately touched by several of the men before a flight attendant discovered the situation and reseated the girl.

Though disconcerting, the use of commercial airlines to deport illegal immigrants is not unique to the United States. Many western European nations also use the same system, although they are more likely than the United States to escort the deportee to the final destination. The simple fact that deportees are being forced to return against their will to a place they wanted to get away from automatically puts them in the category of potential attacker—regardless of a criminal background or not. Many illegal immigrants have risked life and limb to enter the United States and can understandably be quite upset when they are compelled to return to their home country. Some may face prison or political retribution or worse. Others might simply not want to face the shame of coming home a failure. As a result, these "passengers" may feel they have little or nothing to lose in creating a disturbance.

Although every commercial flight that carries deportees presents a clear, high-risk vulnerability, the risk is even greater on small, regional aircraft that typically travel with one flight attendant, but often with none. Because of the lack of a formidable cabin presence, the flight crew is unable to monitor and control what happens in the cabin and may be the last to know if a problem has erupted.

In the wake of the 9/11 attacks, the INS, under orders from the Justice Department, has paid particular attention to rounding up illegal Arab nationals. By the end of 2002, an estimated nine thousand Arab nationals living illegally in the United States were being readied for deportation under the INS policy of unescorted and unrestrained. All nineteen of the 9/11 hijackers were Arab nationals, and three of them had been in the United States illegally. Regardless of nationality, illegal aliens being deported on commercial carriers should be monitored during the flight.

## Lack of Preparation for an
## In-flight Chemical or Biological Attack

Given today's threating environment, preparations must be taken to reduce the possibility that an aircraft could be hijacked or compromised through the onboard release of a biological or chemical agent that would disable both crew and passengers. The installation of full-vision oxygen masks for use by cockpit crews in the event of such an attack in all commercial aircraft would enable the plane to land safely during a chemical/biological attack. Further, air detection systems that alert pilots of the presence of a chemical or biological agent would assist crews in landing the plane without it being hijacked. Although such measures would not help the passengers on the aircraft, it would prevent the plane from being taken over and used as a flying missile on a ground target.

## Failure to Better Control Laptops and
## Other Electronic Devices During Flight

Even though it has been known for years that cellular phones and laptop computers emit low-level interference to an aircraft's guidance systems, no monitors for such radio emissions exist during flight. One of the most vulnerable avionics is the plane's guide slope system, which calculates the angle of descent and helps the pilot land smoothly. If a terrorist reconfigured a laptop computer's basic circuitry, which could be used to send out electromagnetic signals to disrupt the guidance system, the pilot would probably never know. Instead, pilots rely on passengers to turn off their devices, especially during critical moments such as takeoff and landing.

In 1996, the FAA funded a feasibility study to look into ways of detecting interfering signals inside aircraft cabins. A Massachusetts company, Megawave Corporation, was hired to develop a system that scans for a broad range of radio emissions inside the cabin, via sensors mounted above each passenger seat. Megawave's device was successfully tested, but neither the FAA nor the TSA have ever taken the project any further.

## Lack of Global Aviation Security Standards

Since the 9/11 attacks, many within the industry have come to believe that the greatest vulnerability to the system lies with the lack of common international security standards. In many corners of the world, countries are playing by their own rules when it comes to aviation security. At a large number of the world's airports, the bare minimum of security seems to be the rule. In many places, decisions on what equipment to buy have become too often influenced by local manufacturing and economic conditions rather than best practice.

In the European Union, bickering among the Netherlands, Austria, Finland, and Germany have delayed plans for the systematic screening of airport staff when they enter secure areas. Divisions over financing are mainly to blame. Loyola de Palacio, transport commissioner for the EU says, "There is a great dispute over the need for additional aviation security, which many member states refuse to pay."[1] One reason may be the fact that aviation standards in the European Union before September 11, 2001, were generally acknowledged to be higher than those in the United States because of increased measures taken after the 1989 Pan Am 103 explosion over Lockerbie, Scotland.

Nevertheless, several glaring vulnerabilities of the European system have come to light recently and refocused attention on the global aspect of aviation security. In September 2002, for example, a massive criminal conspiracy that allowed hundreds of passengers to board flights illegally at London's Heathrow prompted calls for a massive review of security at British airports. A ten-month-long investigation uncovered evidence of a highly sophisticated and global operation that helped immigrants from Afghanistan, Pakistan, Iraq, and Lebanon to travel to the United States and Canada via Britain.

The scheme began when members of a criminal gang with valid tickets, passports, and luggage presented themselves to the check-in desk. These bogus passengers had no intention of traveling; but they received a small fee for obtaining a genuine boarding card. This was then passed along to the illegal immigrant. Under the policy that was exploited, passengers only needed to show a security boarding card when they passed from check-in to the departure lounge. Passports were not even checked.

Once the illegal passenger had made his way to the flight, private security guards employed by the airlines were supposed to check boarding passes and passports to make sure the person who checked in was the same person presenting himself at the gate. It was those guards who were bribed to allow passengers to pass through unchecked. The guards would get a call about a week in advance telling them which passengers to look out for. Although up to four guards worked each gate, only one corrupt officer needed to be on duty for everything to work smoothly. The illegal travelers would be told to make sure they presented their documents to the guard with a beard or the one not wearing a jacket. Once onboard the aircraft, the travelers were to destroy all documentation showing that they had traveled from Heathrow to prevent suspicion falling on the airport.[2]

## Airspace Violations of General Aviation Aircraft

In the year following the 9/11 attacks, the FAA released a report that said 157 airplanes had violated the airspace over three presidential residences. FAA records showed that planes had flown into off-limits airspace near the White House 7 times; over the presidential retreat at Camp David, Maryland, 104 times; and over President Bush's ranch in Crawford, Texas, 46 times.[3] In an address to airline pilots, Art Cummings, chief of the FBI's National Joint Strategic Assessment and Warning Section, cautioned, "We've seen terrorist organizations looking at everything as small as ultralights to deliver weapons of mass destruction. . . . That's another vulnerability that we have to take a look at very strongly. We have to fill that gap."[4]

In July 2002, USA Today reported that security remained almost nonexistent at forty-five hundred small airports where private planes fly, despite recognition of the risk. As a response, the TSA warned private-plane owners and operators to strengthen security in the wake of credible indications of a terrorist threat. The only advice, however, was weak at best: lock airplanes when not in use.[5]

## Crop Dusters

Although this book has focused primarily on commercial air transport, terrorists and criminals have in the past used other types of aviation to inflict violence as well. One vulnerability that stands out after the 9/11 attacks is the use of crop duster aircraft for diabolical purposes. Mohammed Atta, the reported ringleader of the hijackers, is now known to have tried to learn everything he could about crop dusters. Zacarias Moussaoui, the alleged twentieth hijacker, was found with a crop dusting manual in his possession after he was arrested.

Assuming Al Qaeda wasn't looking to just dust crops, the questions then begs, what drew Atta and Moussaoui to crop dusters? Richard Mueller, a physics professor at the University of California at Berkeley thinks he may have the answer: gasoline. Mueller believes that Al Qaeda was attracted to crop dusters for the same reason they chose fully fueled transcontinental flights on September 11. As a scientist, Mueller realizes that gasoline, when mixed with air, releases fifteen times as much energy as an equal weight of TNT. He says that an Air Tractor 502 crop duster airplane is far smaller than a Boeing 767, the weapon of choice on 9/11, but still can be used as a flying tanker. It has fertilizer containers that hold roughly 300 gallons of liquid, plus a 125-gallon fuel tank. It flies close to the ground, where it can't be seen by most radar. Filling up with 425 gallons of gasoline, the plane is carrying roughly 2.1 to 2.4 tons, the energy equivalent of 32 to 36 tons of TNT.[6]

## Theft of Flight Crew Uniforms and Credentials

In the months after September 11, 2001, it was revealed by the FBI that suspected terrorists had been breaking into the hotel rooms of flight crews and stealing crew uniforms both in the United States and around the world with increasing frequency. Captain Steve Luckey, chairman of the Airline Pilots Association's national security committee said that terrorists "could . . . manufacture a series of uniforms so they could outfit a crew or they could steal enough of them to outfit a crew."[7] In addition, pilots have been warned that "Mideastern-looking males and females" were discovered watching flight crews at hotels, restaurants, and bars in London, Amsterdam, and Frankfurt.[8] These, of course, could simply be families traveling together. But in light of 9/11, suspicions are easily raised.

The vulnerability caused by theft of uniforms aside, there has for a long time been concern that personal information and licenses are far too accessible to outsiders. In 2000, the FAA decided to put the names and addresses of pilots in databases accessible on the World Wide Web. This information could be used in any number of malicious ways. The FAA issues its pilot licenses as traditional paper-and-ink documents that can be easily duplicated or forged. At the time of this writing, neither of these issues had been addressed.

## Inadequate Training for Flight Attendants

Flight attendants are increasingly becoming the last line of defense between the cabin and in-flight assaults and hijackings. With the pilots staying for the most part behind the cockpit door, flight attendants have come to rely more upon themselves, their colleagues, and, in some cases, the assistance of passengers to deal with an in-flight situation.

It is a known fact within the industry that, depending on the carrier, the quality of security training by the airlines is poor and outdated. The training before 9/11 included showing crewmembers videos that focused on hijackings from the 1970s. Unfortunately, the training isn't much better today. Airline security training must not only be more current, it must also address all the threats that a crew is likely to encounter from a terrorist, criminal, or disruptive passenger. But too often the training is minimal and myopic.

Nearly a year after the 9/11 attacks, the Association of Flight Attendants surveyed twenty-six airlines and found that training for flight crews ranged from two to sixteen hours. Sometimes the training involved little more than lectures or video tapes. One training program even taught "verbal judo" designed to redirect behavior through language.[9]

The reason the airlines and not the TSA are responsible for training flight crews comes from the legislation passed in November 2001. ATSA gave the airlines a dreat deal of latitude in setting up the programs for their employees. The training guidelines provided to airlines within the legislation were vague. The vast majority of training programs from the airlines reflected these inadequacies. On September 3, 2002, Dawn Deeks, spokeswoman for the Association of Flight Attendants, observed, "We're really no more prepared to defend ourselves and to defend our passengers than we were on the morning of September 11, 2001."[10]

## USING VULNERABILITIES TO ASSESS RISK

Clearly, several books could be filled with the vulnerabilities that exist within the aviation security system. The key to making risk analysis work is to assess the amount of risk posed by a particular vulnerability or set of vulnerabilities. In industry, the highest risk threats are paired and ranked with the highest risk vulnerabilities that are most likely to occur. Then, we rank the marginal risk threats with the marginal risk vulnerabilities, followed by low-risk threats with low-risk vulnerabilities, etc. This enables us to allocate our resources in such a way that leads us to better manage risk and ultimately better secure the system. Typically, the probability levels of an undesired event are paired with the severity levels of that same event.

## Probability Levels of an Undesired Event

| Probability level | Characteristics |
| --- | --- |
| **A** Frequent | Likely to occur frequently |
| **B** Probable | Will occur several times |
| **C** Occasional | Likely to occur sometime |
| **D** Remote | Unlikely but possible to occur |
| **E** Improbable | Highly unlikely |

## Severity Levels of an Undesired Event

| Severity level | Characteristics |
| --- | --- |
| **1** Catastrophic | Death, system loss |
| **2** Critical | Severe injury, major system damage |
| **3** Marginal | Minor injury, minor system damage |
| **4** Remote | Isolated injury, isolated system damage |
| **5** Negligible | Less than minor injury |

Now let us place these threats and vulnerabilities into a risk assessment matrix.

# TABLE 6. RISK ASSESSMENT MATRIX

**Probability of Occurrence**      **Severity Level**

| | I<br>Catastrophic | 2<br>Critical | 3<br>Marginal | 4<br>Negligible |
|---|---|---|---|---|
| A Frequent | IA | 2A | 3A | 4A |
| B Probable | IB | 2B | 3B | 4B |
| C Occasional | IC | 2C | 3C | 4C |
| D Negligible | ID | 2D | 3D | 4D |
| E Improbable | IE | 2E | 3E | 4E |

Finally, we rate the risk level of a potential event.

**Risk Level**

| | |
|---|---|
| Unacceptable (reduce risk through countermeasures) | IA, IB, IC, 2A, 2B, 3A |
| Undesirable (management evaluation required) | ID, 2C, 2D, 3B, 3C |
| Acceptable with constant management attention | IE, 2E, 3D, 3E, 4A, 4B |
| Acceptable without review | 4C, 4D, 4E |

We need to do this kind of risk assessment in order to paint a clear picture of what the system is confronting. Too often in aviation security, however, planners have used the cookbook approach: mix in a few countermeasures and assume all of a sudden everybody is safe and secure. That is, until the next tragedy. When that happens, as it always will, we throw in a couple more countermeasures in response. And then we wait for the next tragedy to occur.

This is, in essence, surrendering to the bad guys. Acting this way is tantamount to giving up. It's as if to say, "We can't deal effectively with what confronts us, so therefore, we'll never confront it." This is a vicious cycle that if not changed will continue to yield waste, inefficiency, and, at the end, more insecurity. Understanding what the threats and vulnerabilities are and the level of risk they represent is the *only* way that we can deal with the inevitabilities that air transport presents.

# CHAPTER 10

# AVIATION SECURITY MEASURES

"We are what we repeatedly do."

—Aristotle

**B**efore moving forward, let's recall the five elements of the aviation security system. We have discussed four of them at length:

✈ Airports, aircraft, passengers, employees, and other stake-holders need protection. These are the parts of the aviation system that have to be protected.

✈ Strategic objectives are designed to secure the system. In a perfect world, these objectives would meld with the needs of all of the stakeholders of the air transport system. However, it is evident that not all the stakeholders have been well represented in the development of aviation security policy.

✈ Dangerous groups and individuals—both internal and external—seek to inflict damage and violence on the system. These include terrorists, criminals, and disruptive passengers.

✈ Inherent vulnerabilities exist within the system that threatening perpetrators seek to exploit to accomplish their ends. Not all vulnerabilities are equal. Therefore, an attack against one or more vulnerabilities needs to be evaluated based on the potential severity of the attack.

The fifth element, which will be described in this chapter, is:

✈ Security measures are implemented to protect the system's critical parts.

Aviation security, operating as a dynamic system, evolves over time. Strategic objectives may change; threats may change; discovered vulnerabilities may change; and, as a result, security measures must change in response. Effectively implementing aviation security measures requires an evolutionary systems approach. Security measures need to be advanced in a methodical, not scattershot, manner to ensure an appropriate level of aviation security. Improving the overall quality of security measures is enhanced by frequent feedback from *all* of the stakeholders of the air transport system—something the TSA has not been keen on doing since its inception. Like the FAA before it, many believe the TSA is ultimately compromising its goals in favor of industry demands. When the TSA was first formed, Transportation Secretary Mineta outlined three guiding principles of the new agency. Two of them framed security measures in terms of protection and efficiency: "no waiting, no delay" for passengers, and "no danger, no delay" for cargo screening.[1]

Skeptics abound when it comes to the TSA's dual missions of security and service. Bob Monetti, president of The Victims of Pan Am Flight 103 and a member of the Aviation Security Advisory Committee, asked, "Where is service mandated in the Aviation and Transportation Security Act? Equating service and security is like the FAA's problem of trying to promote and regulate. Only in this case, service is not part of the TSA's legislated mandate. It's not in the law. Yes, security has to be aware of customer service, but the reason we had the 9/11 attacks was because security was subordinated to service. It's like no one died on 9/11."[2]

A major challenge in protecting the aviation system is illustrated by the aphorism, "A chain is only as strong as its weakest link." Consider the following as examples of this:

- ✈ Recently, several airports chose to implement a more stringent airport security measure using high-tech ID cards and access codes. In several cases, an airport employee was terminated. The Information Technology department, notified by the employee's manager, delayed removing the employee's access code and ID badge from the system because its policies required notification from Human Resources. Human Resources failed to notify IT, believing that department notification was adequate. In the meantime, the fired and now bitter employee still had access to secure areas at the airport.

- ✈ Layer upon layer of regulations, policies, and hardware are implemented to secure the cockpit door. However, the simple the idea of keeping the door always closed during flight is not practiced or even considered.

- ✈ Most airports around the country use passwords to limit access to secure areas. But many fail to train employees to stop "piggybacking," that is, to not follow a person through a secure door. Each person should always be responsible for only his or her entry.

- ✈ More and more air marshals are deployed to protect flights. Nevertheless, in the rush to increase the number of air marshals, the training standards have been diluted. Air marshals are given only the minimum requirements and training to do their job. For example, how to distinguish between a disruptive passenger and a terrorist is rarely taught to the trainees. In the meantime, new and untried air marshals have overre-

acted to low-risk circumstances, thereby exposing themselves and their firearms to the terrorists.

✈ Checkpoint screeners are trained to better detect prohibited
items. However, they are not taught to be on the lookout for
lead-lined film bags that, if not detected, can transport any
illegal weapon through the checkpoint.

These examples demonstrate the need to take a holistic systems approach to aviation security. The evidence is compelling
that neither technologies nor policies alone really offer strong aviation security. Theft of cargo and baggage takes place despite the
screening of employees and the restriction of access to secure
areas. Prohibited weapons flow through checkpoints despite
better-trained, better-paid, and more observant workers. To best
manage the risks posed by threats to the aviation system, a comprehensive approach to aviation security needs to be created; one
that embraces both human and technical dimensions, and one that
is not wholly subservient to the needs and wishes of a few stakeholders within the system, i.e., the executives of the airlines.

## WHERE TO PUT OUR RESOURCES?

Effective aviation security measures represent a combination of
activities and techniques that increase the system's deterrence, prevention, and detection. Given that aviation security resources are
finite, and that security measures must be carried out within the
context of other constraints, it is not possible to "buy" security by
implementing all available measures. The TSA tried to do this in the
first few months of its existence but, instead, it ran out of money,
scared away passengers, and nearly crippled several airlines.

Trade-offs must be made and, consequently, there needs to be
a strategy in place to determine which security measures are to be
employed and how. This is where the risk analysis and assessment

approach provides real value, because it provides a guide for using finite resources and directing them to the places that represent the highest threat to the system's vulnerabilities.

In the previous chapter, it was determined that the events that present an unacceptable level of risk were the ones that had the following severity levels: frequent and catastrophic; probable and catastrophic; occasional and catastrophic; frequent and critical; probable and critical; and frequent and marginal. To reduce these risks, security measures must be enacted. Preventing these threats and attacks are where our resources should be dedicated.

# THE PURPOSE OF AVIATION SECURITY MEASURES

The perpetrators of violence—terrorists, criminals, or disruptive passengers—act against the system in several ways. Threatening individuals or groups may pose different levels of danger. The severity of the perpetrators' attacks are thus variable. The severity of an attack by a drug courier or an upset passenger who didn't get an upgrade, for instance, is not nearly as strong as a determined terrorist whose mission is to sacrifice his life to bring down an airliner.

Resources of the perpetrator vary as well. Different perpetrators use various resources, including skills, tools, motivation, and opportunity. The use of these resources can increase or decrease as a function of time. In response to the resources of potential perpetrators, three kinds of aviation security countermeasures should be implemented:

✈ Security measures that reduce the severity of the threat
✈ Security measures that reduce the persistence of the threat
✈ Security measures that reduce value loss to the system

## Reducing the Severity of the Threat

Any action, mechanism, device, program, or policy that reduces the severity of a threat can be classified as a security measure. For instance, a large percentage of air-rage cases—approximately 40 percent—involve alcohol abuse, and nearly half of those cases stem from passengers transporting and drinking their own booze on board. A measure—in this case, a law—that prohibits the consumption of alcohol from one's own supply while on an aircraft may substantially lower the persistence of the threat of a drunken, disruptive passenger. Though the measure may have an initial effect of lowering the persistence of the threat, without prosecution of offenders the effectiveness of the restriction may diminish. A more effective measure may be to publicize the law by providing a sign placed behind the ticket counter or at the jetway, thus providing a better basis for prosecution.

## Reducing the Persistence of the Threat

Another type of security measure is one that increases the system's resistance to a perpetrator's particular mode of attack. The classic policy of limiting control to secure areas by using passwords and identifications is an example. Such measures can improve the system's resistance to certain types of attacks by simply making it more difficult to penetrate secure areas. This often deters a potential attacker and may force him or her to explore another mode of attack at a different point of the system.

## Reducing Value Loss to the System

The third type of security measure reduces the value loss associated with an adverse event. Security measures that work by detecting threats can be thought of as reducing value loss. For example, a terrorist tries to pass through a security checkpoint with a firearm. An effective security measure to deter this type of attack is to detect the weapon and react to it before it passes through. If it is not found at the checkpoint, maybe another screening before boarding will discover it. Or, possibly, a random bag check at the gate might as well. Nevertheless, the extent and amount of possible loss increases the longer that the weapon goes undetected.

The characteristics of the security measure itself also are important. Any security measure has to be set up properly, be tamper resistant, and work whenever it is required. The degree to which these three characteristics are met contributes to the resistance of the security measure against a potential perpetrator's mode of attack.

Certainly, there are security measures that are more effective mechanisms against certain types of attacks than others. By using risk analysis and assessment tools, we can determine which measures to put where in order to best anticipate threats and attacks. Unfortunately, the vast majority of measures put in place in response to the 9/11 attacks have not been implemented with this notion in mind. For instance, dedicating resources to shaking down old people, former Vice President Al Gore, and even Attorney General John Ashcroft at security checkpoints may appeal to our sense of fairness and equality, but it does nothing to reduce the risks that invariably menace the system. In fact, it may actually increase levels of *insecurity* by shifting valuable resources away from the real threats.

# EVALUATING AVIATION SECURITY MEASURES

The creation of the Transportation Security Administration and the aggressive schedule Congress set up to improve aviation security has ratcheted up demand for companies that can offer security-related services and products to the government. With billions of dollars to be spent in the coming years, businesses of all shapes and sizes with any kind of security technology are bidding for the government's business. And, because of ongoing threats and fears, often verging on paranoia, about terrorism, the government is listening.

Recently, it seems everybody is being asked to get on the government spending train. Almost daily headlines suggest that some technology is the magic bullet that will make everyone safer. In the realm of aviation security technology, trusted-traveler programs, biometrics, and million-dollar machines designed to screen checked luggage for explosives are promoted as the salvation America is seeking. More and more, passengers are asked to accept aviation security decisions carte blanche and pay for them as well. Measures such as biometrics and trusted traveler cards intrude into the area of civil liberties and may actually compromise our rights as Americans. Unfortunately, however, most of us have little or no idea how to evaluate whether these security measures are ultimately worth the cost or not.

Bruce Schneier, a noted author and security information expert, has developed a five-step series of questions to determine whether a security measure is really any good.[3] His series of questions should be used to assess any aviation security measure in place or under consideration today.

1. *What problem does the security measure solve?*
2. *How well does the security measure solve the problem?*
3. *What other problems does the security measure cause?* Security is a complex and interrelated system; you change one thing and the effects ripple.
4. *What are the economic and social costs?* Costs are not just financial, they're social as well. Sometimes a security measure, even though it may be effective, is not worth the costs.
5. *Given the above, is it worth the costs?* This is the easy step, but far too often no one bothers to figure it out. It's not enough

for a security measure to be effective. We don't have infinite resources. We don't have infinite patience. As a society, we need to do the things that make the most sense, and that are the most effective use of our security dollar.

There are aviation security measures that pass this test. Increasing the number of prohibited items allowed on aircraft was a good idea. So was conducting more extensive background checks on airport and airline workers. Reinforcing the cockpit door was a good first step to making things safer. However, it became a problem when the new door didn't stay closed.

Again, for obvious reasons, the intent here is not to spell out the strengths, weaknesses, and shortcomings of every aviation security measure that has been or is being considered for implementation. Instead, the following pages are dedicated to encouraging broader thought and discussion about the overall state of aviation security in today's environment. To best accomplish this, it is necessary to provide concrete examples to illustrate the point that most security measures, especially those that hype the latest technologies, too often neglect the most severe risks. Several post-9/11 measures have come up short in reaching their objectives and they deserve our attention here: explosives detection systems, biometrics, and the trusted traveler program. The point is to provide relevant examples of how security measures should be evaluated. If this is not done properly, the measure can retard the level of security and quite possibly reduce it. It can also misdirect valuable resources that could be better spent elsewhere.

## Explosives Detection Systems

One of the key components of the ATSA was its December 31, 2001, deadline to scan all checked baggage for bombs. This deadline was under attack almost from the moment the president signed the bill into law. The airlines, airports, passenger groups, and other important constituencies within the industry were skeptical of several aspects of the mandate—including the machines that were chosen by the government to screen the baggage.

Despite almost universal criticism of its selected explosives detection systems (EDS), the TSA continued to buy thousands of machines that used the suspect technology to meet a near-impossible deadline. At the center of the controversy is the contention that the hundreds of millions of dollars spent on EDS baggage-screening machines—as large as a small truck, each costing nearly $1 million—was not well spent since some are reputedly not capable of detecting explosives.[4] In many ways, the technology seems flawed.

Using X rays, experts have repeatedly said that the EDS machines defy scientific logic. They note that X radiation is, by its very nature, intrinsically incapable of detecting explosives. It is a density-sensitive but chemically blind technology. The X-ray machines are able to produce precise three-dimensional images of dense objects but cannot tell their chemical contents. This is true even of the most precise X-ray detectors, the ones that the TSA uses as EDS. In the jargon of security professionals, X rays, like metal detectors, are only "anomaly detectors." They flag the suspicious objects as "possible explosives," which triggers an alarm and, in turn, should require the opening of the luggage for manual inspection.

In fact, it is argued that none of the thousands of X-ray monitors at the 450 or so U.S. airports has ever detected an explosive. The X-ray detectors are essentially prolific false-alarm generators. The false-alarm rate depends entirely on how you determine that an object is "suspicious." In most X-ray systems, this life-or-death decision is left to the subjective judgment of the operator. If you want to be strict in order to diminish the chance of missing a real explosive (to minimize the so-called "missing fraction"), you end up with 100 percent false alarms and jamming of the checkpoints throughout the system. If, on the other hand, you want to reduce the false alarms by relaxing the "suspicious" criteria, you increase the chance of a bomb sneaking through.

More advanced systems try to compensate for the chemical impotence of X rays via the surrogate devices that respond to the density, size, and other anticipated features of explosives. Small incremental improvements in false-alarm rates can be made at a great cost, especially in increasing the amount of time it would take to check each piece of luggage. Still, the chemically blind anomaly detectors such as X rays are and always will remain a probability game, more akin to gambling than an exact science. It is like teaching a computer-aided blind person to recognize colors in an oil painting.

There is a clear and immediate need for a "sniffer"—a chemically specific explosives detector that would remotely and noninvasively determine, without opening the suitcase, whether or not an anomaly is or contains an explosive. A logical response of TSA to the security demand for a chemical sniffer would be a massive scientific effort to develop chemically specific detection methodologies. Instead, it is perpetuating an anachronism: X radiation, a nineteenth-century technology, is stretched into the twenty-first century as the panacea in diagnostics.[5]

Charles Slepian says, "The technology they're using does not work, that much we do know. They're too slow, and they mistake tubs of jam for explosives. Credible evidence suggests they can't find explosives very well."[6]

Using the criteria set out earlier, let's evaluate EDS as a security measure:

1. *What problem does the security measure solve?* To be frank, using EDS machines does not solve very much.
2. *How well does the security measure solve the problem?* Given the current state of the technology, EDS barely scratches the surface when it comes to addressing the issue of screening checked bags for bombs.
3. *What other problems does the security measure cause?* In addition to the increased burden and costs to airports, air car-

Explosives detection systems (EDS) were rushed into place by the TSA after 9/11. Using antiquated nineteenth-century X-ray technology, machines like this one have a false-positive rate of about 25 percent.

riers, and passengers, the insecurity of the EDS machines perpetuate the very real possibility of a bomb being placed in the luggage hold of an aircraft.

4. *What are the economic and social costs?* The incredible financial costs notwithstanding, the false sense of security such a measure creates can lead only to further breaches of the system.

5. *Given the above, is it worth the costs?* No, not at all.

Consider the following scenario that involves exploiting the new weaknesses caused by the use of current EDS technology. Assuming that the goal of terrorism is to deliver terror, bringing down an airplane is not the only way to cripple the aviation system. One way that this can be done is to load up a suitcase with fifty or sixty pounds of high explosives. Some tactical packing would be required to disguise some elements of the firing train, but that wouldn't be hard at all. Then, choose an airport that uses the L-3 EDS machine, which requires little or no operator input, so that being sneaky isn't so difficult.

While waiting at the terminal, a little surveillance could be done to determine how often the EDS machine is loaded up and how the bags are handled. It would be really easy to conduct the surveillance at Baltimore-Washington International (BWI) because the airport has placed chairs right in front of the EDS machines so you can sip on a Starbucks and act like you're reading the paper. The suitcases could be wired for three different kind of detonations using a barometric device, a timer, and a trip.

The best time to do this would be around Thanksgiving or Christmas when the terminals are packed with passengers, offering a potentially high body count and a means of cover and concealment. Once the bag is introduced into the check baggage screening system, it would be time to slowly and carefully slip away, unless you are a suicide bomber.

If the bag passes through the EDS machine unscathed, the barometric device or timer would detonate the suitcase and be certain to take out the airplane (on the ground or in the air) or in the baggage make-up area, which would be a great place for an explosion because at most airports it is usually contained in an area directly beneath the terminal.

If the EDS machine happened to detect the explosives, there's a good chance the operator would let it go because it was just another false alarm. If the operator did decide to check the bag, he or she might swab the outside of it to check for any traces of explosives. A smart terrorist, who would have been able to observe this while seated at BWI for example, would most certainly have taken precautions to cleanse the outside of the bag before checking it. If the EDS operator decided to open the bag, the trip would set off the explosives. Detonating fifty or sixty pounds of a high explosive in a crowded concourse would turn every nearby object, including the massive EDS machine, into tons of flying shrapnel that would slice through the bodies of people hundreds of feet away. Thousands of people could be maimed, injured, or killed.

Now let's say that the machine catches the explosives and the operator decides not to open it, but instead calls the bomb squad. After X-raying the bag and discovering the explosives, the bomb squad decides to evacuate the terminal and call in responder teams to handle the situation. With thousands of people waiting outside on the sidewalk or grass, a second terrorist drives a truck bomb into an area full of passengers, airport employees, and emergency response personnel and detonates it. . . .

## Biometrics

Biometrics is the science and technology of measuring and statistically analyzing biological data. In aviation security, biometrics usually refers to technologies for measuring and analyzing human body characteristics such as fingerprints, eye retinas and irises, voice patterns, facial patterns, and hand measurements—especially for authentication purposes that give access to secure areas. Often seen in futuristic science-fiction adventure movies, face pattern matchers and body scanners are likely soon to emerge as replacements for computer passwords.

Fingerprint and other biometric devices consist of (1) a reader or scanning device; (2) software that converts the scanned information into digital form; and (3) a database that stores the biometric data for comparison with previous records. When converting the biometric input, the software identifies specific points of data as match points. The match points are processed using an algorithm into a value that can be compared with biometric data scanned when a user tries to gain access. Fingerprint, facial, or other biometric data can also be placed on a "smart card" and users can present both the smart card and their fingerprints or faces to merchants, banks, or telephones for an extra degree of authentication.

Although it had been in use in a number of industries for years, biometrics was one of those measures that was "born again" as a viable aviation security measure after the September 11 attacks. Many thought biometrics could control the airport workforce problem. In addition, supporters of biometrics argued that passengers and other airport visitors could also be more easily monitored to help insure that "bad people" are kept away from places they shouldn't be.

However, airports across the country are known to have inconsistent standards, uneven oversight, poor enforcement, and multiple constituencies from local to national authorities when it comes to monitoring airport workers. As a result, opportunities exist for unauthorized individuals to compromise the integrity of the workforce through the use of false identification, prohibited presence in secure areas, and piggybacking.[7] Face-scanning technology was touted by manufacturers as the perfect device for recognizing terrorists in airports. In theory, the measure uses surveillance cameras to scan crowds for bad guys and sound an alarm when a match is made between a live person and the system's database of known criminals. A few months after the 9/11 attacks, the federal government and technology companies rolled out a series of testing programs at airports around the country to prove its worth.[8]

Nevertheless, several tests conducted during the first part of 2002 revealed that the use of biometrics may not be a practical tool for airport security. During a ninety-day test at Boston's Logan International, passengers and airport workers were scanned as they passed through a security checkpoint. Their images were sent to a computer that compared the images to pictures stored in its memory. Passengers and airport workers whose faces matched those on a watch list were examined again by screeners, who compared their faces to pictures displayed on a computer screen.[9]

Test results revealed that the measure could be fooled when individuals turned their heads in certain directions. It was learned just holding one's head at an unusual angle threw the computer off. In addition, to make the measure more effective, the testers calibrated it more loosely, so that it would signal anybody whose face had even a slight resemblance to a face on the computer's watch list. At that setting, most passengers and airport workers were identified as possible matches. Because of the huge number of possibilities, it was discovered that the system put so much stress on their human operators that airports would have to hire more screeners to run them. Some estimates even said that an operator would need to take a break every twenty minutes.

There are other concerns about the use of biometrics as well. Privacy concerns abound with regard to the gathering and sharing of biometric data. One suggestion to assuage those with privacy concerns is to encrypt biometric data when it's gathered and discard the original data to prevent identity theft. However, this may still give too much power to the entity that gathered the original data.

Another concern is that the ability to circumvent the system is not very hard to do. In Japan, a scientist named Tsutomu Matsumoto decided to see how easy it could be to fool the system. Matsumoto, along with his students at Yokahama National University, showed the system could be tricked with a little ingenuity and ten dollars' worth of household items.

Matsumoto used gelatin, the stuff that Gummi Bears are made out of. First he took a live finger and made a plastic mold. (The mold is the kind that is used to make plastic molds and is often found at hobby shops). Then he poured liquid gelatin into the mold and let it harden. (The gelatin comes in sheets and can be purchased at any grocery store.) This gelatin fake finger fooled fingerprint detectors about 80 percent of the time.[9]

Using the criteria set out earlier, let's evaluate biometrics as an aviation security measure (we'll see the answers are pretty much the same as those for EDS):

1. *What problem does the security measure solve?* Using biometrics doesn't solve much of anything.
2. *How well does the security measure solve the problem?* Given the current state of the technology, biometrics barely scratches the surface when it comes to addressing the issue of airport and aircraft access.
3. *What other problems does the security measure cause?* In addition to the increased burden and cost to airports, air carriers, and passengers, the insecurity of biometrics perpetuates the very real possibility of a "bad person" gaining access to a prohibited area.
4. *What are the economic and social costs?* The incredible financial costs notwithstanding, the false sense of security such a measure creates can lead only to further breaches of the system.
5. *Given the above, is it worth the costs?* No, not at all.

## The Trusted Traveler Program

To ease the movement of more passengers through security checkpoints at airports, the TSA has been looking at what is being called the "trusted traveler program." The idea is founded on the notion that randomly screening individuals is a waste of time and resources, one that compromises the effectiveness of the new security measures. Every security resource tied up in extra scrutiny of a frequent flier or a little old lady or a Congressman is a resource not dedicated to the unknown passenger pool.

The trusted traveler program would be available to flyers who choose to submit to extensive background checks by the government. Once cleared, these travelers would be issued a card carrying a photo along with a thumb or palm print or, perhaps, the result of a biometric retinal scan. Trusted travelers would show the card at security checkpoints and receive only cursory screening, similar to what passengers experienced prior to 9/11. Proponents argue that the program would benefit everyone else by allowing screeners to focus most of their effort on passengers whose backgrounds have not been checked. The airlines have been pushing the program heavily on Capitol Hill. They expect better business if passengers, especially those who travel often and typically pay higher fares, had a way to avoid the more intensive and time-delaying personal inspections.

But what happens if a registered traveler ID is issued to the wrong person? Even assuming the databases contain 100 percent accurate service, what criteria would be used to determine if someone really deserves to be a registered traveler? We really don't know.

Registered traveler ID cards could well become extremely coveted by terrorists and criminals. Some of these groups would be willing to recruit and prepare operatives who remained law-abiding and dormant for years, to place terrorist sleepers in a position to obtain those nifty ID cards.

All the fancy computerized trusted traveler systems won't tell you if the person holding the card is a would-be terrorist who successfully qualified for registered status. He could be all-American, too. Oklahoma City bomber and decorated Gulf War veteran Timothy McVeigh and alleged D.C. sniper and Army veteran John Muhammad might well have qualified for a registered traveler card. Even just one error in handing out these IDs—if it permits a terrorist to pass through airport security with a lesser degree of security—could be catastrophic.[10]

Using the criteria set out earlier, let's evaluate the trusted traveler program as an aviation security measure (we'll see the answers are pretty much the same as those for EDS and biometrics):

1. *What problem does the security measure solve?* Using the trusted traveler wouldn't do much to help stop "bad people" from gaining access to secure areas.

2. *How well does the security measure solve the problem?* Given the concerns about the need for perfection, trusted traveler IDs may actually raise the vulnerabilities caused by airport and aircraft access.

3. *What other problems does the security measure cause?* In addition to the increased burden and cost to airports, air carriers, and passengers, the insecurity of the trusted traveler program perpetuates the very real possibility of a "bad person" gaining access to a prohibited area.

4. *What are the economic and social costs?* The incredible financial costs notwithstanding, the false sense of security such a measure creates can lead only to further breaches of the system.

5. *Given the above, is it worth the costs?* No, not at all.

Clearly, I chose these security measures to make a point. That is, by the government failing to evaluate each security measure fully, we are left pretty much in the dark as to how that measure will ultimately impact the entire system. Only by taking a holistic approach can we better understand the intricate relationships that develop within the aviation security system and whether they need modification or not. Either way, taking the extra step of a full-fledged assessment is the only way we can ultimately determine the real value to the system and to its users.

# CHAPTER 11
# MAKING SENSE OF IT ALL

"Security can only be achieved through constant change, through discarding old ideas that have outlived their usefulness, and adapting others to current facts."

—William O. Douglas

Imagine the following: At a sparsely attended Saturday morning press conference, the TSA reportedly announced it was seeking to address what it called "the number one threat to airline security." According to the spokesman, who refused to give his real name, the agency was prepared to consider banning certain passengers on all domestic and international flights. "In every single breach of security in recent years, whether it was an act of terrorism or some other form of crime or disruptive behavior, it was a passenger who subverted the safety systems on board the aircraft or in the airport. Even threats that came back in the form of explosives inside baggage were eventually traced back to a ticketed individual. As great a revenue source as they have been, passengers simply represent too great a risk to the airline industry."[1]

Under the proposed reforms, the TSA would institute a strict ban on all adult passengers, passengers eighteen and under, international travelers, and domestic customers. A series of questions and ID checks would be used to determine whether the individual is a pilot, flight attendant, or air marshal—the only humans who would be allowed to board an aircraft flying within or headed for the U.S.

In what appeared to be a last resort aimed at curbing rising frustration from dealing with aviation security, the spokesman said, "Frankly, we've tried everything else. We've put up more metal detectors, searched carry-on baggage, and prohibited passengers from traveling with sharp objects. Yet passengers still somehow continue to find ways to breach security. Clearly, the passengers have to go."

He added, "We realize that these new regulations would, for many air travelers, be a major inconvenience. But we at TSA feel that it's a small price to pay to ensure the safety of our skies."

Many within the agency seemed certain that while the ATSA provided for several stiff measures to make security better, it still wasn't enough. A high-ranking TSA official who declined to go on the record said this was the last best hope for insuring that another 9/11 didn't happen again. "Federalized checkpoint screeners, fortified cockpit doors, and more plainclothes air marshals aboard planes—all new measures put in place since 9/11—could not eliminate the possibility of another September 11 with 100 percent certainty. This will."

Waving his finger in the air, the official declared, "We've tried every possible alternative, but nothing has worked. For all our efforts, we keep coming back to the same central problem: humans."

Although this was a satire, aviation insecurity will remain a fundamental reality for as long as human beings are associated with air travel and transport. The system will be breached. Terrorists will again kill people on aircraft and in airports as well as elsewhere. Criminals will use the aviation system to steal, murder, and commit sabotage. Disruptive passengers will continue to act out and threaten the safety of others. There is nothing we can do; no amount of risk analysis; no litany of security measures we can put in place; no amount of money will stop *all* the attacks on the aviation system.

If we've learned anything, it is that we must try our best to *manage* the inherent realities associated with the aviation system. Instead of trying to avoid every possible attack, it is incumbent for us to effectively direct our limited resources in ways that will provide the best possible protection. But to do this, we have to get through the false thinking that has dominated much of the post–9/11 aviation security thinking. We cannot guard against every contingency. We cannot spend our way to security. We cannot expect that the next generation of technology will be the magic bullet. We will never be able to stop every prohibited item from getting through the security checkpoints. We will never be able to guarantee for certain that a bomb is not planted on board an aircraft. We will never be able to profile every terrorist or criminal and keep all of them off commercial aircraft.

We have to accept the security risks that naturally come along with having a complex system like commercial aviation. Good aviation security, like good human beings, is not perfect. Nor does it have to be. Aviation security only has to do as well as it can to manage the inherent risks that air transport presents.

This may be much easier said than done. Americans, more than almost all other people on earth, find it hard to accurately evaluate and accept risks. Everything, it seems, from lawsuits to the labels on coffee cups ("Warning: the beverage you are about to enjoy is extremely hot.") and even political pronouncements often suggest it is possible to avoid danger altogether. The 9/11 attacks were meant for millions of Americans to realize that they weren't so protected from terrorism, whether it was on the ground or in the skies. They simply did not know how to evaluate something they had never seen before. In the aftermath of 9/11, individual citizens and the federal government—in their desire for 100-percent security— tend to exaggerate the more spectacular but low-probability risks, while they continue to underestimate more common risks, such as criminal sabotage or disruptive passengers.

One of the most important lessons learned from September 11 is that everyone has a stake in aviation security, regardless of whether they fly or not. Fresh questions continue to be raised about the issue of aviation security. Glaring weaknesses and vulnerabilities exist. Threat levels remain high and everybody seems to be waiting for the next shoe to drop. A battle of imaginations is at hand. How can we outthink, outmaneuver, and outsurprise those who seek to inflict damage on the system?

> Surprise, when it happens to a government, is likely to be a complicated, diffuse, bureaucratic thing. It includes neglect of responsibility but also responsibility so poorly defined or so ambiguously delegated that action gets lost. It includes gaps in intelligence, but also intelligence that, like a string of pearls too precious to wear, is too sensitive to give to those who need it. It includes the alarm that fails to work, but also the alarm that has gone off so often it has been disconnected. It includes the unalert watchman, but also the one who knows he'll be chewed out by his superior if he gets higher authority out of bed. It includes the contingencies that occur to no one, but also those that everyone assumes somebody else is taking care of. It includes straightforward procrastination, but also decisions protracted by internal disagreement. It includes, in addition, the inability of individual human beings to rise to the occasion until they are sure it is the occasion— which is usually too late. (Unlike movies, real life provides no musical background to tip us off to the climax.) Finally, as at Pearl Harbor [and on September 11, 2001], surprise may include some measure of genuine novelty introduced by the enemy, and possibly some sheer bad luck.[2] (brackets mine)

Terrorists and criminals have always had and will continue to possess the upper hand over the aviation security system. Terrorists and criminals are able to decide when and where they will strike. On the other hand, those who practice aviation security must constantly be on alert. The bad guys have to be lucky only once, while the system has to be lucky all the time.

## THE EL AL EXAMPLE

Much interest has swirled around the notion that El Al has the best practices for aviation security in the world and that American airlines have much to learn from them. Many believe that if the United States could mirror what the Israel does, we would be able to reduce immensely the amount of aviation insecurity. For a moment, let's look at how at how a passenger traveling on El Al deals with security.

For a flight departing from Tel Aviv's Ben Gurion International Airport, a traveler is required to arrive three hours before the scheduled departure. As you enter the airport grounds in a car, bus, or taxi, the vehicle is thoroughly searched by uniformed guards armed with submachine guns. Upon approach to the terminal, you'll notice plainclothes security guards stationed at airport entrances and others patrolling outside the terminal in loose-fitting jackets that cover bulging weapon holsters. Cars are prevented from making more than momentary stops to unload passengers and luggage.

Once inside, you'll be subjected to rigorous and time-consuming questioning. Many of the questions are perfunctory: "Who packed your bags?"; "When did you book your flight?"; "What is the purpose of your travels?; "Who paid for your tickets?"; "Do you have any weapons?" The interrogators are not very interested in your response. What they are really looking for are evasive answers or any sign that you might be hiding something. Trained professionals all carefully study your tone of voice, mood, and body language. Passengers can be questioned by up to three different screeners separately. The process allows guards to quickly spot and profile those who appear nervous or suspicious. While most Israeli Jews quickly pass through the questioning phase, Arabs and certain foreigners are singled out for the most intense grilling.

There's a good chance your luggage will be opened and carefully inspected down to the contents of the smallest toothpaste tube, before you check in. Sophisticated high-tech explosives detection equipment, unlike the dubious stuff being used in the United States, is used to examine all luggage. While similar scanning equipment is used for spot checks at several European airports, no other airline requires as many luggage scans as El Al.

The security measures continue after check-in. Only passengers with tickets and boarding passes are permitted to take the escalator to the departure lounge. Metal detectors and additional questioning await the passenger before boarding the aircraft. Departures are often delayed because security has to remove checked bags belonging to passengers who did not board the plane within the allotted amount of time. If checked bags are transferring from another airline to El Al, they have to be checked through security again. Other delays may occur due to cargo problems. To make sure that there are no explosives that can be set off by a barometric fuse sensitive to altitude, El Al places all of its cargo in decompression chambers before takeoff.

Once on the plane, a passenger is quite aware of the presence of several armed air marshals on the flight. In addition, El Al cockpits are sealed off by two virtually impenetrable doors, which are *never* opened during the flight. Pilots, although they are veterans of the Israeli Air Force and are trained in handling weapons and in hand-to-hand combat, do not carry guns in the cockpit.

Although El Al's security system is comprehensive and well designed to mitigate risk (El Al hasn't had a terrorist incident in more than thirty years), it is important to recognize that such a system may not be realistic for an airline industry as large as that of the United States. El Al has forty daily flights and carries about

3 million passengers a year. In the United States, there are approximately twenty-seven thousand flights a day and more than 600 million passengers flying every year. Nevertheless, there are several things we can learn from the way El Al approaches security, as outlined below.

## Some Aviation Security Imperatives

In his book, *Strange Victory: Hitler's Conquest of France,* Ernest May analyzed why the vaunted Maginot Line, the chain of fortifications on France's border with Germany, fell in 1940 to the invading Nazis within a few short weeks. Its similarities to the present aviation security system ring true.

> The Maginot Line was indicative of the faith that technology could substitute for manpower. It was the forerunner of the strategic bomber, the guided missile, and the 'smart bomb.' The same faith led to France's building tanks with thicker armor and bigger guns than German tanks had. But having machines do the work of men carried a price in slowed down reaction times and lessened initiative for battlefield commanders.

We cannot build a Maginot Line in our nation's airports that is so expensive and difficult to navigate that its raises the costs so high—both socially and economically—that the industry is permanently damaged. In many ways, this may have already happened. The visceral decisions and bad planning related to aviation security after the 9/11 attacks have caused serious injury to an already wounded industry. Tens of millions of passengers continue to stay away, leaving plenty of empty airline seats. We have to look at aviation security through a different set of eyes, in many ways as the Israelis do.

*Intelligence Is the Best Weapon*

The most powerful weapon against terrorists and criminals is intelligence. Physical security measures are generally of limited use when it comes to battling the bad guys. Unfortunately, the history of aviation security has tended to favor measures over intelligence in every sense of the word. Even more upsetting, as we've seen, these measures are often reactive to the threat environment and designed to stop an attack that has already occurred. They are neither proactive nor well thought out.

A traveler's journey from the entrance of an international airport to an airplane seat offers a concise history of air terrorism and the *reactive* measures designed to stop it. When checking in, you will be asked whether you packed your luggage yourself, because in 1986 at London's Heathrow Airport, an Irish woman carried ten pounds of explosives in a suitcase, placed there without her knowledge by her Palestinian boyfriend. Your carry-on will be screened for guns or other weapons, because armed Palestinian guerrillas took control of an El Al flight from Tel Aviv to Rome in 1968. The airport staff you meet will have been subjected to rigorous background checks, because the radical Islamic hijackers of a TWA flight from Athens in 1985 used aircraft cleaning personnel to smuggle guns on board. If you never end up boarding the plane, your luggage will be removed from the cargo hold, because an unclaimed bag aboard a Pan Am flight in 1998 blew up the aircraft over Lockerbie, Scotland.[3]

In today's world, intelligence is essential in countering criminals and terrorists and diminishing their tactical effects and strategies. Moreover, the threat of large-scale acts of terror and the use of weapons of mass destruction increases the need to prevent and foil dangerous schemes and give warning before such acts occur. However, the existence of small groups and cells of highly motivated extremists and fanatics, who in many cases act without direct orders from others, create a formidable group of enemies.

Penetrating and infiltrating these groups is highly difficult. Nevertheless, without a comprehensive, sagacious, and firm policy of conducting intelligence, terrorists and criminals will continue to present a very real threat to the future of the aviation system.

### Put the Primary Focus on Bad People Instead of Bad Things

Since its creation, the TSA has overwhelmingly focused on keeping bad things out of airports and off aircraft. This is simply the wrong approach. If we are to do our best to provide the vital public service of aviation security, we must design processes that are people-centered. Aviation is a human endeavor. The threats to the system come from human beings. The vulnerabilities are human creations. An airport is a city with three neighborhoods: the landside, the terminal, and the ramp. To do the best job possible to protect the system, we must know the residents of each of those areas as well as who is visiting the city. We must look more at keeping bad people away from airports and aircraft than anything else, while balancing individual rights and supporting the Constitution.

### Profiling Is to Some Degree Necessary

The need to look at certain passengers differently than others from a security perspective only makes sense. A World War II veteran simply does not pose the same level of potential threat as a young man traveling from a troubled country. To try to argue this point is silly. Therefore, measures should be in place that profile those passengers who do provide a higher level of threat.

### Minimize Access Where Possible

Every time you block access to something, it becomes one less way an attacker has to get at the system. However, restricting access goes only so far. We have to allow passengers, flight crews, mechanics, ramp workers, security workers, and dozens of other groups a certain amount of access to aircraft and sensitive areas of the airport so that the system can function. Airports, by and large, are designed to handle tens of thousands or even hundreds of thousands of passengers and employees every day. This helps to ensure that the transportation of people and cargo can move efficiently and safely around our country and the world. This makes our lives easier and better. Managing accessibility, like managing risk, is what needs to de done.

## SOME FINAL THOUGHTS ON RISK ANALYSIS AND ASSESSMENT

The risk analysis and assessment system is simple enough to enable its use without necessitating a level of expertise that may take decades to acquire. This approach enables security to be driven into more areas of the system and to become more devolved. At the same time, it allows those who perform the daily function of aviation security to have a much clearer sense of what is happening.

Risk analysis not only directs appropriate information to each stakeholder involved in delivering aviation security, but it can also play a major and proactive role in enhancing the understanding of each stakeholder's needs. The process of risk analysis and assessment brings often divergent and separated groups closer together so that they can function better as a single team or system.

Risk analysis allows security to be properly targeted to the highest probability of severe threats and existing vulnerabilities. We cannot protect everything from a potential attack. Nor should we try. Failure to understand this will inevitably result in further unnecessary expenditures and heavier burdens on the industry. Risk analysis promotes far better targeting of dangers and it facilitates appropriate security decisions in a much more logical manner than any other method.

Risk analysis is the best way to understand the overall risk posed to the aviation system. It allows us to identify those risks that are easily reduced or eliminated and to clarify what is known and not known about what we are confronting. Additional security almost always involves additional costs. As aviation security does not generate income, it is important that it is justified in financial as well as social terms. The risk analysis process directly and automatically generates such justification, placing all the security recommendations within the context of the threats and vulnerabilities to the entire system. At the end of the day, risk assessment provides the most consistent and objective approach to all aviation security decisions.

In many ways, we are in a situation where risk management is no longer a potential option. In a highly fluid environment, where threats and vulnerabilities are constantly evolving, we simply cannot afford to have costly or inappropriate security. Effective risk management can be nothing less than the defense of the aviation industry as well as the foundation of our nation's security.

# AFTERWORD

As a professional author, I am keenly aware of the need to always write to a specific audience. My earlier books on globalization, entrepreneurship, and leadership were clearly targeted to a definable group of potential readers, mostly within the business community. My book on disruptive passengers was a leap outside of that comfort zone and was written for the much broader audience of air travelers.

The intended readers for this book are my children. I'm still not exactly sure what individuals or demographics will be interested in what I have put forth in the preceding pages. I hope many thousands of people will be intrigued by what I have detailed here. I wish that my ideas on aviation security will be debated and even criticized so as to further the discussion on the way we will protect aviation in the coming years. If they don't, I'll take my lumps, swallow my pride, and move on to the next project.

From the beginning, I felt the story about how our government let us down and continues to do so when it comes to aviation security needed to be written for future generations to understand what really went on before and immediately after the attacks of September 11, 2001. The jury is still out as to whether anyone within the government will ever be held personally responsible for their role in creating policies that contributed to the events of that horrific day. Always an optimist, I believe the truth will one day win out. It just may take a little longer than I might expect.

*No accountability, no justice, no progress.*

# APPENDICES

# KEY AVIATION SECURITY DOCUMENTS

## EXECUTIVE SUMMARY
## September 11, 2001

On September 11, 2001, several commercial air carrier incidents, believed to be terrorist-related, occurred in various locations in the United States. As numerous U.S. passenger air carriers were involved, this has impacted many passengers as well as numerous persons on the ground in these various crash sites. The following is a summary of the events, which have occurred:

American Airlines Flight 11, departed today from Boston Logan International Airport (BOS), bound for Los Angeles International Airport (LAX). The aircraft type was a Boeing 767-200 with eighty-one passengers, nine flight attendants and two crew in the cockpit, which totaled 92 persons on this flight. At approximately 9:18 a.m., it was reported that the two crew members in the cockpit were stabbed. The flight then descended with no communication from the flight crew members. The American Airlines FAA Principal Security Inspector (PSI) was notified by Suzanne Clark of American Airlines Corporate Headquarters, that an on board flight attendant contacted American Airlines Operations Center and informed that a passenger located in seat 10B shot and killed a passenger in seat 9B at 9:20 a.m. The passenger killed was Daniel Lewin, shot by passenger Satam Al Suqami. One bullet was reported to have been fired. The flight headed in the direction of John F. Kennedy International Airport (JFK). At 9:25 a.m., this flight crashed directly into one of the towers at the World Trade Center. At 11:26 a.m., a passenger manifest was obtained. The status of any selectees is as yet undetermined.

United Airlines Flight 93 departed this morning, from Newark International Airport (EWR) bound for San Francisco International Airport (SFO). The aircraft type is Boeing 757, confirmation pending. The flight consisted of thirty-eight passengers, two pilots and five crew members, which totaled 45 persons on this flight. Two selectee passengers (Christine Adams and Nicole Miller) were boarded on this flight with no unusual behavior noted per the air carrier personnel and screeners. No cargo was on board this flight. One unit load device (ULD), was on board containing U.S. mail. At 9:42 a.m., there was a report of a bomb threat on board this flight. Passengers' screams were heard in the cabin. At 10:05 a.m.; the Illinois State Police received a 9-1-1 telephone call from a passenger on that flight, who reported three hijackers were on board with knives and reportedly made a bomb threat. The three hijackers were reported to be rushing to the cockpit area. At 10:12 a.m., the flight crashed near Sommerset, PA. This location is approximately 70-90 miles from Pittsburgh near Route 30.

United Airlines Flight 175, departed from Boston-Logan International Airport (BOS), bound for Los Angeles International Airport (LAX). This aircraft type was a Boeing 767. There were no selectee passengers on this flight. The flight consisted of nine crew members and forty-seven passengers, which totaled fifty-six persons on this flight. At 9:30 a.m., radar contact with FAA air traffic control was lost. At 9:43 a.m., United Airlines reported that one flight attendant was stabbed and two crew members were killed. This flight crashed directly into the second World Trade Center Tower.

9/11/01 5:31 PM.

American Airlines Flight 77, departed Washington-Dulles International Airport (IAD), destined for Los Angeles International Airport (LAX). This flight departed Gate D26 of the IAD mid-field terminal at 8:09 a.m., and was airborne at 8:21 a.m. The aircraft type was a Boeing 757. Number of selectee passengers is unknown at this time; ramp personnel noticed two selectee checked bags on the ramp. One non-selectee passenger did not board due to confusion of gate location. This flight consisted of fifty-eight passengers and six flight crew members, which totaled sixty-four persons on this flight. There was no cargo being transported on this aircraft. There were a total of thirty-five checked bags. It is presumed that this flight crashed into the Pentagon located in Washington, D.C. at approximately 10:06 a.m.

Additional information is continuously being gathered on each of the four incidents described above.

ORDER:                      8400.10

APPENDIX:                   4

BULLETIN TYPE:              Flight Standards Information
                            Bulletin for Air Transportation
                            (FSAT)

BULLETIN NUMBER:            FSAT 97-01

BULLETIN TITLE:             Miscellaneous NTSB Cabin Safety
                            Recommendations

EFFECTIVE DATE:             01-07-97

TRACKING NUMBER:            A-96-85, A-96-84, A-96-88

1.  PURPOSE.  This bulletin responds to three National Transportation Safety Board (NTSB) recommendations, which are discussed individually in the attached appendices.

A. Appendix 1 addresses NTSB recommendation A-96-85, which asks the Federal Aviation Administration (FAA) to require that each flight attendant have a cockpit key in his/her possession at all times, while on duty.

B. Appendix 2 addresses NTSB recommendation A-96-84, that asks the FAA to provide guidance to the air carriers regarding the implementation of the requirement that occupants, who are more than 24 months old, be restrained during takeoffs, landings, and during turbulence.

C. Appendix 3 addresses NTSB recommendation A-96-88, that asks the FAA to provide information to air carriers regarding flight attendant's attire.

2.  ACTION.  Principal operations inspectors (POI) are requested to ensure that the information contained in this bulletin is made available to their assigned air carriers.

3.  INQUIRIES.  This FSAT was developed by AFS-203.  Persons making inquiries should call AFS-203, at 202-267-3735.

4.  EXPIRATION.  This bulletin will remain in effect until January 31, 1998.

\s\
David R. Harrington
Manager, Air Transportation Division

Attachments

APPENDIX 1.

This appendix addresses NTSB recommendation A-96-85.

1.  BACKGROUND.  During a recent accident, the pilots received information that they had an engine fire when the right engine fire warning light illuminated. However, the most timely and unambiguous information that there was a fire inside the airplane was provided by the flight

attendants. The flight attendants did not follow the airline's procedure that required the use of the interphone emergency signal to inform the cockpit of the fire. One of the flight attendants in the forward section of the cabin saw flames around the flight attendant in the aft jumpseat and tried to notify the flight crew of the fire by opening the cockpit door. As required by FAA regulations, the cockpit door was locked. While one of the forward flight attendants reached for the cockpit door key, which was stored in accordance with the carrier's procedures, the other flight attendant successfully opened the cockpit door with her own key, and informed the flightcrew of the fire.

A. Because of the need for a flight attendant to retrieve a cockpit key from its assigned storage area before being able to unlock the cockpit door, the use of the chime signal would probably have been the faster way to notify the cockpit about the fire. However, the Safety Board has some concerns regarding the use of the interphone as the sole means of notifying the cockpit of an onboard fire. In an emergency situation, the cockpit crew may be too busy with other emergency tasks to immediately answer the interphone. In fact, the Safety Board has investigated accidents in which the flight attendant's interphone calls were not answered. In this particular instance, however, it was fortunate that one of the flight attendants had her own cockpit key, and thus was able to quickly notify the flightcrew about the fire.

B. The Safety Board is concerned that having only one cockpit key available and stored in a prearranged area, may not allow a key to be readily accessible to all flight attendants in an emergency. Also, relying solely on the chime emergency signal to be answered by the flightcrew in the cockpit, when they may be preoccupied with other emergency procedures and tasks, could result in the flightcrew not becoming aware as soon as possible that a fire exists in the cabin. The Safety Board concludes that all flight attendants should be able to quickly access the cockpit when appropriate. Therefore, the Safety Board believes that the FAA should require that each flight attendant have a cockpit key in his/her possession at all times, while on duty.

C. Title 14 of the Code of Federal Regulations (14 CFR) part 121, section 121.313 (g), stipulates that there must be a key for each door that separates a passenger compartment from another compartment that has emergency exit provisions. The key must be readily available for each crewmember. In addition, 14 CFR part 121, section 121.587, stipulates that the cockpit door must be locked during flight. "Flight" has been interpreted for purposes of this regulation as when the airplane moves down the runway for purposes of flight. The communication method of choice between the cabin and cockpit is use of the interphone, however, this is not always successful. When the interphone cannot be used, then communication directly with the flight crewmembers by opening the cockpit door may be the only method available. Therefore, each crewmember should know how to open the cockpit door. Many airlines accomplish this by issuing each crewmember a cockpit key and ensuring that the crewmember has a cockpit key with him/her at all times. Other airlines feel that having the cockpit key in the possession of each flight attendant could pose a security risk, and therefore stores a key in a place convenient to the cockpit. In addition, to ensure that each crewmember has a cockpit key readily available and is trained on the availability and use of the cockpit key, most airlines have a "back-up" method of gaining admittance to the cockpit. This "back-up" method is usually a pre-arranged signal, which alerts flight crewmembers so they can open the cockpit door.

2. POLICY. The cockpit key is not available to the flight attendants if they cannot easily locate and retrieve it. Therefore, air carriers should either ensure that each flight attendant has a cockpit key in his/her possession during the performance of duties in flight, or that a cockpit key is in a readily accessible place on the aircraft and flight attendants are trained in this location during initial and recurrent training. In addition, air carriers should emphasize to crewmembers the importance of using the interphone. Also, air carriers should consider establishing a pre-arranged signal for admittance to the cockpit, to be used in cases where the cockpit key, for some reason, is not available.

APPENDIX 2.

Appendix 2 addresses NTSB Recommendation A-96-84.

1. BACKGROUND. During a recent NTSB accident investigation, it was determined that one child more than 24 months old was listed as a lap child, despite regulations that require all passengers more than 24 months old to be restrained during takeoffs and landings. The Safety Board has long been concerned about the inadequacy and enforcement of this regulation, and in the last several years, has identified at least six accidents and one enforcement action, in which children more than 2 years old, were unrestrained because they were held in someone's lap. The ages of these children ranged from 26 months to 5 years old.

2. POLICY. Present regulations allow parents/guardians of children under two years of age the option of holding these children in the lap. Children over two years of age must be restrained in an approved restraint device. This restraint device may be an adult passenger seat/seat belt, or an approved child restraint system. As pointed out in the background to the NTSB recommendation, the problem appears to be that some parents/guardians want to hold children who are more than two years old in their lap. This is not an

acceptable procedure. In order, to preclude this occurrence, many airlines ask the age of the lap-held child when it is presented to be placed on the load manifest. In addition, many airlines instruct crewmembers to ask parents the age of lap held children. These procedures complement each other and are recommended.

APPENDIX 3.

This appendix responds to NTSB Recommendation A-96-88.

1. BACKGROUND. The NTSB investigation of a recent accident disclosed that the flight attendant who received the most serious injuries was wearing shorts and a short-sleeved shirt. Safety experts agree that in order to decrease the

chance of sustaining burns, it is better to wear long
sleeves and pants, than it is to wear short sleeves and
short pants.  In addition, fabrics such as wool and
cotton are better than synthetic fabrics.  Also, it is
better to have low heel shoes which are enclosed, and straps
or laces are encouraged while sandals are discouraged.

2.  POLICY.  Air carriers should ensure that those charged
with developing the criteria for crewmembers' attire, while
performing duty associated with flight, are aware of these
safety considerations.  In addition, air carriers should
ensure that crewmembers are aware of the information
regarding the safety considerations for the apparel they
wear during flights.

U.S. Department
of Transportation

Federal Aviation
Administration

# Memorandum

---

Subject:  __ACTION:__ Selection of CASFO Manager          Date:  AUG 1 3 1998

From:  Manager, Civil Aviation Security Division,          Reply to
       ANE-700                                             Attn. Of:

To:  Associate Administrator for Civil Aviation
     Security, ACS-1,
     THRU: Director, Office of Civil Aviation Security
     Operations, ACO-1

I am providing this memorandum for concurrence of selection for the position of Manager, Boston Civil Aviation Security Field Office. **I have selected Mary Carol Turano as the new Manager.**

There were four persons who applied for the position. The applicants were Daniel L. Furlong, Stephen Luongo, Jim Powers, and Mary Carol Turano. The Human Resource Management Division did not refer Jim Powers because he did not meet the qualifications.

The qualified applicants were interviewed on July 31. They were interviewed by a three person panel that included Ernie Landry, Manager, Human Resources Management Division, ANE-10; Stacy Grace, Federal Security Manager at Ronald Reagan National Airport; and Joyce Scott, Manager, Chicago Civil Aviation Security Field Office. This was a structured interview and all three applicants were asked identical questions. There were a total of 15 questions.

Each applicant was asked a question by a panel member and allowed the opportunity to respond. The applicant's responses were rated as either effective or ineffective based on pre-established criteria. Once the interviews were completed, the interview panel provided me a written summary report of their observations. The panel advised me that all three applicants interviewed well, with Mary Carol Turano having the most effective responses.

The interview panel members stated they were very impressed with Mary Carol Turano. The panel indicated that Mary Carol Turano demonstrated a high energy level and she showed lots of enthusiasm throughout the process. The panel was also impressed when Mary Carol Turano stated how she prepared for the interview. She stated that she recognized she had some weaknesses in the Air Security Program, so she spent some time at the airport with the Federal Security Manager at Dulles International Airport. There she was able to become familiar with a number of areas that are the responsibility of a Civil Aviation Security Field Office.

I contacted some of Mary Carol Turano's previous supervisors, who all spoke well of her and of her ability to adapt quickly. It was indicated that she will work extremely hard to get her job accomplished. I feel confident she will do so as well.

I recognize Mary Carol Turano does not currently have extensive program knowledge in Air Security Issues, but I know she will be a quick learner. Mary Carol Turano demonstrates good people skills, which I feel is needed with a young workforce. The Boston Civil Aviation Security Field Office has a very young and inexperienced workforce and Mary Carol's energy will assist in making them one of the most productive in the country. The CASFO Manager reports directly to me, therefore, I will be able to provide the necessary mentoring and coaching to assist her in learning this new position. I strongly feel that Mary Carol Turano will quickly become a valuable asset to the division.

Based on the application package, the interview, and my supervisory inquiry, Mary Carol Turano is the best of the applicants for this position. This applicant currently resides in Washington D.C. and will require a Permanent Change of Station (PCS).

If there are any questions, please do not hesitate to call me.

Willie J. Gropper, Jr.

May 7, 2001


The Honorable John F. Kerry
304 Russell Senate Office Building
Washington, DC 20510


Dear Senator Kerry,


There was a very disturbing investigative report last night (Sunday evening May 6) on Channel 25 FOX News at 10PM regarding airport security. Although the report focused on Logan Airport and TF Green in Rhode Island, as a recently retired FAA Special Agent, I know this is a national problem, not one simply unique to New England Region. I've asked my friend Steve Elson, another former FAA Special Agent, to forward a video copy of the report to you. Both of us are willing to testify before Congress should the need arise and we are both committed to doing whatever is necessary to improving our aviation security system. We are hopeful that you would show the video to your peers, Senator McCain and members of any House committee dealing with aviation security.

The FAA does everything it can to prevent news reports of this nature under the guise of it being a public safety issue, which should not be given a public forum. Unfortunately, this report once again demonstrated what every FAA line agent already knows, the airport passenger screening system simply doesn't work as intended. The FAA would prefer to continue to promulgate a façade of security, than to honestly assess the system. Management knows how ineffective the current system is, but continues to tell Congress that our airport screening is an effective deterrent.

FAA officials point to a 95+% success rate of FAA screening checkpoint tests, particularly when reassuring the flying public and Congress. They do this even though they know that every time a Red Team, or news reporter in this instance, tests the system, the exact opposite occurs with a failure rate of 95+%. The difference is realistic testing versus tests designed to avoid enforcement litigation problems with the airlines. It is a clear example of self fulfilling prophecy, whereby the tests are designed to produce a desired outcome, rather than to truly reflect the status of aviation security.

FAA management will point to a decline in incidents of hijacking since the system was put into effect in the '70s. My question is, "Have they kept up with the times?" Do you see a horde of Cuban exiles just waiting to commit air piracy to return to Havana? Or, has the threat become more refined over the years? I've stood along the Potomac and watched our big air ships fly in low and slow along the river. What protection is there against a rogue terrorist with a Stinger missile? While the FAA has focused on screening for handguns, new threats have emerged, such as chemical and biological weapons. Do you really think a screener could detect a bottle of liquid explosive, small battery and detonator in your carry on baggage? And with the concept of Jihad, do you think it would be difficult for a determined terrorist to get on a plane and destroy himself and all other passengers? The answers to these questions are obvious.

The FAA was dubbed "The Tombstone Agency" by Mary Schiavo, the former DOT OIG. The reason is that the agency never seems to act until there has been an air tragedy. Think for a moment how vital the air transportation industry is to our overall economic well being as a nation. Think what the result would be of a coordinated attack which took down several domestic flights on the same day. The problem is that with our current screening system, this is more than possible. Given time, considering current threats, and it is almost likely. We don't have to wait for a tragedy to occur to act. There are simple, cost effective means to improve the system now.

The DOT OIG has become an ineffective overseer of the FAA, particularly since Mary Schiavo's departure. Scathing reports have been developed on airport/airline security and FAA facility security. Still, the culture continues to perpetuate itself and managers have been promoted up the chain, despite the fact that they've supported this façade of security and abused line agents who dare to speak the truth. The answer here is not to fire a few hapless low paid screeners or continue to issue meaningless fines against the airlines. The answer is to change the prevailing culture within Civil Aviation Security at the FAA from one concerned with continuing to support the façade, to one committed to protecting the traveling public. Let our agents do their job. Don't stifle initiative and independent thought and observations. Don't continue to silence those who refuse to buy the party line and actually attempt to reveal the façade.

It is time for the truth to be known, before an incident occurs. It is not in the best interests of public safety to continue this façade of security. Hopefully, FOX 25 will distribute this report to all its national affiliates and encourage similar testing. National TV news magazines could also help bring focus. Perhaps we can force a public forum where line agents could testify before Congress and finally secure an honest assessment of aviation security, as well as some positive change.

Thank you,

Brian F. Sullivan
FAA Spec Agent (Ret)

This space
Is for
Pagination
And allows
For
The
Masthead

Subject: **ACTION**: Compliance and enforcement philosophy

Date: May 30, 2001

From: Associate Administrator for Civil
Aviation Security, ACS-1

Reply to Attn. of: Bryan
202-267-8592

To: Managers, Civil Aviation Security
Divisions 700's, Federal
Security Managers

As we work with the aviation industry, it is important to remember that our primary goal as a regulatory agency is to gain compliance. While I know there are circumstances that present difficult choices, it would be helpful to explain our approach to compliance and enforcement issues.

As I outlined in the ACS strategic plan, the safety and security of the flying public will depend upon the FAA and industry maintaining a candid, respectful, and mutually responsive business relationship. To be effective in this relationship, we need to be flexible. While I expect regulated parties to comply with regulatory requirements, there will be times when we find areas of noncompliance. When we do, I want to fully consider the actions the party has taken to fix the problem. I want to work with industry to develop action plans to permanently correct problems that have resulted in violations. To encourage industry to join us in this effort I do not expect us to impose a civil penalty against a regulated party for certain unaggravated violations, if we believe the party has successfully implemented a permanent fix that will resolve the security problem and preclude recurrence of future violations. To answer questions you may have about this new philosophy and how it will work, detailed guidance will be provided to you shortly.

I want to continue to give our partners a realistic opportunity to comply with the regulations and to work with us.

Signed
Michael A. Canavan

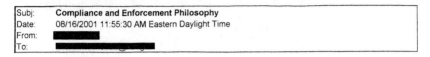

## Appendix F. August 16, 2001, E-mail from Brian Sullivan to Michael Canavan, FAA Associate Administrator for Civil Aviation Security to FAA Federal Security

| Subj: | Compliance and Enforcement Philosophy |
|---|---|
| Date: | 08/16/2001 11:55:30 AM Eastern Daylight Time |
| From: | ▓▓▓▓▓▓ |
| To: | ▓▓▓▓▓▓▓▓▓▓▓▓▓ |

General,

Your C&E philosophy makes sense and is "well intentioned", but is being abused by field management to close cases without finding and as the basis for not opening cases, despite the fact that violations persist.

Your intent was to work with the regulated parties and develop action plans to permanently correct problems. Here's what's really happening. A problem is identified. Instead of opening a case, we work with industry to develop the required plan. The agents go out and find that the problem persists, but field management won't allow them to open a case, incorrectly citing your May-30th memorandum as the basis for their decision. As a result we have a paper fix. Nice looking plans, but no real fix. The facade of security continues. Our line agents continue to experience the frustration of not being allowed to do their jobs.

The only way to confirm what I am saying is to check on the ground. What's the old military saying, "What goes right is what a commander checks", or something like that? When the FOX25 report was done at Logan in May, the reporter went back a few weeks later, after the dust had settled, and re-checked the same screening checkpoints with the same negative result, despite assurances from the BOS CASFO and airport/airlines. I know FOX could easily determine if these current action plans work as intended. Let me suggest that it would be better if you looked at some of these action plans and test them with a red team to see if they actually work. I know our field agents have re-checked violations after the action plans have been developed only to find that the same violation persists. Plans aren't worth the paper they are written on unless they work. The only way to determine if they really work is to test them with an "honest broker"and that can't be done by our line agents, if their management won't open up cases when problems persist.

If you doubt what I'm saying, this is very easy to check. I know you get more with honey than you can with vinegar, but compliance requires both the carrot and the stick, if it is to be truly effective. The industry is primarily concerned with the bottom line ($) and will give security the attention it merits, only if we are perceived as both willing to work with them, while at the same time committed to both compliance and enforcement. If they think we are soft and they can get away with paper plans, that is exactly what they'll do. The key is to insure that the action plans do, in fact, permanently correct the problems which have resulted in violations. That is not happening. When the plans don't correct the problem, we have to have field management willing to open up cases and support our line agents who find that violations persist.

I hope this is helpful information. I'm not looking for a response. I just want to help you make your philosophy work as intended.

Best wishes. We are hearing some good things since your arrival.

Brian Sullivan

| | |
|---|---|
| Subj: | **Re:Compliance and Enforcement Philosophy** |
| Date: | 08/22/2001 12:41:44 PM Eastern Daylight Time |
| *From:* | ███████████████████████████████████ |
| *To:* | ██████████████ |

brian, thanks for the email. from what i have been able to see and hear you ar
right. this is being fixed. mike

**From:** ███████████████████████████
**To:** ███████████████████
**Sent:** Wednesday, September 26, 2001 7:01 PM
**Subject:** Fwd:Future

_____Forward Header_____
Subject:   Future
Author: Michael Canavan
Date:      9/22/2001 5:10 PM

Prior to last week's events there were rumors that I would be moving on to another position in Washington. I want you to know I have no plans to leave and that I am fully committed to instilling the  public's confidence back in our Civil Aviation System. It will take all of us in ACS to do this. You have my committment and I expect yours as we move down the road. ACS's character will be defined as to  what we do after we have been knocked to our knees. Now is the time to do the right things in terms of security which is after all, our "Sense of Purpose." Mike

# Appendix I. Immigration and Naturalization Service Policy for Escorting Illegal Aliens

## STANDARD

## ENFORCEMENT

---

### ESCORTS

I.  **PURPOSE:** This policy establishes guidelines for escorting persons detained under the authority of the Immigration and Nationality Act (INA) by all officers of the Service. Previously issued Immigration and Naturalization Service (INS) policy and guidelines on this subject are superseded by this policy.

This policy applies to all INS personnel who apprehend, take into custody, transport or otherwise detain persons, with or without warrant, as authorized in the INA, as amended and delineated in Title 8, Code of Federal Regulations.

II.  **AUTHORITY:**

Title 8, United States Code, Section 1357 (Section 287, INA), and Title 8, Code of Federal Regulations, Section 287 (8 CFR 287).

III.  **POLICY/STANDARD:**

It shall be Service policy that:

A.  All detainees in INS custody shall be escorted in a manner that is safe, secure, humane, and professional.

B.  All detainees will be escorted in accordance with classifications and procedures found within this standard. No detainee will be transported for any purpose without an assessment performed in accordance with the Use of Restraints standard.

C.  When escorting detainees, especially unaccompanied detainees of the opposite sex or juveniles, in Service vehicles, insofar as technologically possible and resources allow, all officers shall maintain regular radio or telephonic communication with other Service personnel.

D.  No detainee shall be transported without the assigned officer conducting his/her own search of the detainee=s person, except when exigent circumstances pose a safety hazard or danger to the officer, detainee or public. In the latter case, a search shall be conducted as soon as practicable. A pat down search shall be the minimum search conducted. This includes officer-to-officer transfers, as well as transfers from an

---

institution.

E.    Regardless of the means of transportation, no baggage, luggage or parcel shall be transported in a manner making it accessible by any detainee unless the item has been thoroughly searched by the officer transporting the detainee, except when exigent circumstances pose a safety hazard or danger to the officer, detainee or public. In the latter case, a search shall be conducted as soon as practicable.

F.    The passenger section of all empty INS vehicles and immediate confinement areas shall be searched prior to as well as following each escort to ensure that no weapons or contraband have been hidden or left behind.

## IV.    RESPONSIBILITIES:

The Service shall be responsible for identifying and providing approved restraints for use by all officers escorting detainees.

Managers and supervisors are responsible for determining the need for and number of escorts required for any detainee in accordance with this standard and the classification system found in it.

It is the responsibility of supervisors and officers to convey all known information of escape risks, criminal background or involvement, violence or medical indications to escorting officers.

Escorting officers have the responsibility to determine the need and level of restraints used at any time while escorting a detainee.  Such determination shall be based on articulable reason(s).

## V.    DEFINITIONS:

Adult - A male or female person believed to be 18 years of age or older.

Classification Officer - an Immigration Officer designated by a supervisor to determine the escort classification of a detainee.

Contraband - Any item possessed by a detainee which is prohibited by the INS or by law.

Detainee - Any person, regardless of citizenship or nationality, under arrest, detained, restrained, or confined by the INS or any other law enforcement agency.

Escape Risk - Any detainee who, in the belief of an INS officer, may attempt escape from INS custody if not otherwise prevented. An individual who will actively seek opportunities to escape from INS custody.

Escort - To transport or otherwise move any person detained under the laws of the United States.

Immediate Relative - A person being one of the following to a detainee: spouse, parent, grandparent, child, sibling, aunt, uncle, or legal guardian. When applied to a juvenile, the immediate relative must be an adult.

Juvenile - A person known or reasonably believed not to have reached his/her 18th birthday.

Medical professional - A licensed doctor, nurse, practitioner, technician, or aide trained to treat, provide care, administer medication or services specific to the medical needs of the person being escorted.

Pat-down Search - An examination in which an officer's hands briefly make contact with a detainee's body and clothing in order to detect and remove contraband and/or weapons.

Unaccompanied Female - A female not in the company of an immediate relative.

Unaccompanied Juvenile - A juvenile not in the company of an adult immediate relative.

Weapon - Any object, item, or device that may be used to cause physical injury, incapacitate, or diminish capability, temporarily or permanently.

VI.    **PROCEDURES:**

When transported in a vehicle, detainees shall be restrained in accordance with the Use of Restraints Policy and when restrained, placed in seatbelts (when practicable). Depending upon the risk classification of the detainees, duration of travel, and destination, consideration may be given to the use of additional Service-approved restraints.

It is recognized there may be situations, such as emergencies, where only one officer may be available to provide escort service.

Under normal circumstances, apply the procedures below:

A.    Escorts Using INS Sedans, Vans, or Utility Vehicles.

When a lone officer transports an unaccompanied detainee of the opposite sex or an unaccompanied juvenile, he/she shall maintain regular electronic voice communication with a supervisor, radio operator, or other INS personnel at a separate location, insofar as technologically possible. At a minimum, communication shall include the officer's or unit's identity, route of travel, current location, and mileage, as a security precaution. See Standard III C.

1. Unsecured sedan/van/utility vehicle: A lone officer shall not transport more than two detainees in an unsecured vehicle, except when accompanied by other law enforcement vehicles. Two officers may transport no more than the rated capacity of the vehicle permits.

2. Secured sedan/van/utility vehicle: One officer may escort the number of detainees permitted by the vehicle=s rated capacity. Such escorts are permitted provided the officer will not be involved in movement of the detainees outside the vehicle without other assistance. Movements over long distances or time or requiring stops for food or fuel will normally require more than one officer.

B. Movement of Detainees Via INS or Charter Bus. All applicable Department of Transportation laws, rules and regulations will be observed, especially relating to the number of hours a driver may be on duty and rest breaks. In addition to these requirements the following procedures will also be applied:

1. Unsecured bus: There shall be a minimum of two (2) officers on the bus. This may include the driver if both are INS officers. They shall have radio or cellular telephone communication and, if authorized by an Authorizing Official pursuant to the INS Firearms Policy, shall be armed. Officers shall not be armed while in the area where detainees are seated. Depending upon the risk level of the detainees, duration of travel and destination, consideration should be given to the use of additional officers and an escort vehicle.

2. Secured bus: A minimum of two officers shall be used on all escorts; this includes a driver and a security officer. They shall have radio or cellular telephone communication and, if authorized by an Authorizing Official pursuant to the INS Firearms Policy, shall be armed. Officers shall not be armed while in the secured (caged) portion of the vehicle.

   Local V/R runs, using secured buses, within districts or Border Patrol sectors may be exempted from the two-officer requirement so long as the bus is equipped with a Service radio and the route taken permits immediate response to a request for back-up.

3. Family groups, unaccompanied females and unaccompanied juveniles shall be separated from unrelated adult males by separate passenger compartments or an empty row of seats. These detainees shall be transported separately from other detainees, if possible. See Standard III C.

4.   When two or more buses (secured or not) are used together, one escort vehicle and at least two additional officers should be used.

C.   Escorting Detainees on Justice Prisoner & Alien Transportation System (JPATS) Aircraft.

Detainees transported on JPATS aircraft (and vehicles) are subject to the policies and stipulations found in the JPATS Prisoner Transportation Manual. Officers should consult that reference for instructions regarding the use of restraints and escorts on JPATS aircraft.

D.   Escorting Detainees on Commercial Aircraft.

Personnel assigned to making reservations to transport detainees on scheduled commercial aircraft will normally advise the airline(s) one day before the anticipated flight of the intention to transport a detainee under the control of a law enforcement officer. Persons making reservations shall notify the carrier or agent accepting the reservation of each traveler=s escort classification. In accordance with Federal Aviation Administration (FAA) regulations (14 CFR 108), under no circumstances, exigent or otherwise, will this notification take place less than one (1) hour prior to the flight. **Airlines are under no obligation to transport an officer and/or his/her escortee.** Corporate airline policy on the types and use of restraints varies between airlines and airports. The aircraft's captain has the ultimate authority as to who may travel on his/her aircraft and to determine the use of restraining devices on any flight. **If the captain's decision is unacceptable, the officer shall deplane and make other arrangements.**

1.   All detainees shall be classified by a supervisor or classification officer prior to being transported on commercial carriers using the classification system described below. The supervisor shall be required to make an assessment of the detainee using the Service=s classification standards prior to escorting any detainee. Factors considered shall include the detainee=s known criminal background, past behavior, potential risk to the public, medical condition, sex, age and ability to resist an officer=s control of the detainee effectively. Notation of the detainee=s escort classification by category number shall be made on the Record of Persons and Property Transferred, Form I-216, in the margin immediately to the left of each person=s name and AA≅ file number. Absent Form I-216, written record should be made on any local flight arrangements sheet to be permanently retained in the alien=s file. Similarly, the escorting officer=s classification of restraint level should be noted in the same location on the form I-216. See Standard on Use of Restraints.

**When one or more factors indicate greater safety or escape risk, the officer should**

**always exercise discretion in favor of more caution and greater supervision.** Escorts required for a detainee classified using this classification method shall only be counted toward the escort requirements of one group. For example, the two escorts required for a maximum risk alien shall not be calculated toward the requirements of lower risk groups of aliens traveling on the same aircraft, nor vice versa. Lone escorts shall not be used except for those aliens in Group 1a.

| Group Descriptors | Escort Required |
|---|---|
| **Group 1**<br><br>Persons granted or permitted withdrawal of application for admission, or voluntary departure by a Chief Patrol Agent, District Director or an Immigration Judge. This presumes the person has good moral character and no known criminal background or asocial behavior.<br><br>Persons removed pursuant to an order of removal who have no known criminal background or asocial behavior.<br><br>Non-criminal aliens escorted to a point of departure, placed on the carrier and met by other INS officers at the point of arrival. | No escort required. |
| **Group 1a**<br><br>Persons in need of assistance because of age, infirmity, mental capacity, handicap or language barriers.<br><br>Medical parolee en route to half-way house or point of release from INS custody. | Minimum of one escort. |
| Unaccompanied juveniles. | One escort of same sex per juvenile. |
| **Group 2**<br><br>Persons at any time charged or convicted of non-violent crimes, or known to be criminally involved, determined by an INS officer to be non-violent. | A group of fewer than 10 detainees requires no escorts. Minimum of 2 escorts for a group of 10 detainees. Each additional group of 5 requires 1 more escort. |

240

| Group 3 | |
|---|---|
| Persons who are chargeable or were charged or convicted of criminal violations involving threat of force, assault, violence, or killing any person or animal.<br><br>Persons who are or have been verbally abusive, verbally combative, confrontational, vulgar or verbally coercive during the course of their immigration proceedings or custody, or who have otherwise indicated willingness or intent to resist physical removal from the United States pursuant to a lawful order or finding.<br><br>Persons who are serving criminal sentences, being transferred or delivered to other jurisdictions where criminal proceedings are pending, regardless of whether or not the crime underlying the unexpired sentence or proceedings involved force or violence. | At least two escorts per detainee are required. When traveling to destinations within United States, these shall be armed officers. |
| **Group 3a** | |
| Individuals deemed by the U.S. Public Health Service or by competent medical authority to be in need of medical services during travel. | Minimum of two escorts, plus a medical professional. |

2.    The lead escort officer transporting aliens to commercial aircraft shall be responsible for providing the airline=s representative a breakdown of aliens being placed on the flight, by classification type.

3.    All detainees determined to require escort aboard commercial aircraft, i.e., criminals, juveniles, medical cases, and escape risks, shall be processed for the flight with the airline=s gate personnel at least one hour prior to the flight. The officers and detainee(s) should be preboarded and seated in the last row(s) of

the aircraft whenever possible. Airlines may reassign escorted passengers to other seat assignments; however, escorting officers should be seated next to the detainee(s).

4. Officers should use care and discretion when removing restraints from properly classified low risk detainees to avoid notice by the traveling public and airline personnel. Officers should be aware the general public may perceive persons transported to airline gates or boarded in restraints as threats to airline and passenger safety when traveling without escorts.

5. In addition to properly assigning escorts in accordance with this standard and the classifications therein:

a. Criminal juveniles should be escorted consistent with the classification criteria for adult detainees with the same background. See Use of Restraints Standard.

b. Non-criminal juveniles may be escorted by certain designated non-INS personnel under contract or interagency agreement with the INS in place of INS officers.

c. All Federal Aviation Administration regulations pertaining to transporting Amaximum risk≅ individuals in custody of law enforcement officers shall be observed.

d. When making travel arrangements, reasonable efforts must be made to observe individual airline policies regarding the transporting of detainees.

e. At least one escort shall be the same sex as the detainee.

6. Food and beverages:

a. Detainees who require officer escorts shall not be served meals that require metal utensils that could be used as weapons. This information should be conveyed to the carrier when making reservations. Plastic utensils are permissible if the escorting officer determines their composition is such that they do not constitute a threat to the officer=s or the public=s safety.

b. Escorted detainees may not consume alcoholic beverages while in the custody of an INS officer. Likewise, an officer shall not consume alcoholic beverages when escorting detainees nor while carrying a firearm. See AM 20.012. Firearms Policy Standard.

7. Airlines shall be notified of high risk or criminal aliens at the earliest point in the arrangement process. **If there are indications of outside intervention**

**against or on behalf of the detainee, commercial air travel shall not be utilized.** Alternate modes of transportation, such as government aircraft, shall be used.

8. Foreign flights:

a. To Designated Country: Except when foreign laws, regulations, or policies countervail, or international agreements stipulate otherwise, or prior arrangements have been made to transfer custody of a detainee to foreign officials, restraining devices shall be removed after landing and immediately prior to disembarking in the detainee=s designated country of deportation. The individual should be allowed to disembark without restraints.

In situations where, because of restrictions on their use, restraints must be removed before landing in the detainee=s designated country, the responsible supervisor will assure that sufficient officers are assigned to provide for the safety of the officers and the public.

b. Transiting countries en route: Managers, supervisors, and officers should take appropriate steps to familiarize themselves with the applicable rules, regulations, laws and policies relating to the carriage and use of restraints when escorting persons through other countries en route to the escortee=s stipulated country of repatriation. This may require advance notification of both the foreign government and United States officials in the countries anticipated to be transited.

When a removal requires escorts and the use of restraints, and the itinerary requires transiting a third country, arrangements shall only be made to transit countries which permit the use of restraints to execute valid removal orders.

If the person escorted presents a risk to the escorts or the public, and a suitable itinerary using a third country permitting the use of restraints cannot be arranged, JPATS shall be contacted to arrange for either a government or charter aircraft. If JPATS cannot accommodate the removal, Headquarters Office of Field Operations shall be contacted for guidance or authorization to use other means of transportation.

E. Medical Escorts:

1. Consistent with the INS medical policies, and as clinically indicated, a medical professional shall escort a detainee with a minimum of two Service officers. During transport, the medical escort will sit as close to the detainee and INS escort officers as possible. At no time will the medical escort assume security responsibilities for the detainee while in the air or on the ground. Additionally, prescription medication shall be provided only by a medical professional for the treatment of diagnosed illnesses,

e.g., heart disease, depression, or other conditions. Under <u>no</u> circumstances shall detainees be medicated solely to facilitate transport, unless a medical professional determines that they present a danger to themselves or to others. Disposition of medication and related equipment is the responsibility of the medical escort.

2.    In all cases, the detainee shall be accompanied by up-to-date copies of his/her medical records, which shall be carried in a sealed envelope or folder, clearly marked "Medical Records, To Be Opened By Authorized Medical Personnel Only." The detainee shall be accompanied by medical supplies and medication sufficient for the duration of the trip, plus at least three days.

3.    Do not transport detainees who have not been medically screened on commercial aircraft. Those transported on JPATS are subject to stipulations found in the JPATS Prisoner Transport Manual.

F.    Medical Precautions:

Officers should be alert for symptoms such as coughing, fever, sweating and emaciation, in addition to obviously open wounds or bleeding. If an officer suspects that an alien may be infected with a contagious disease, the following precautions should be taken:

1.    Transport the alien in a separate vehicle from other aliens.

2.    Place a surgical mask on the alien.*

3.    Seat the alien in the rear of the vehicle, next to an open window to provide as much ventilation as possible.

*USPHS authorities have advised that a surgical mask is considered adequate for these purposes. A HEPA mask is not necessary.

___ Approved

___ Not approved

---

_____      _____
(Signature)       (Date)

# NOTES

## CHAPTER 1: HOW COULD THIS HAVE HAPPENED?

1. Air Transport Association, *The Economic Impact of Commercial Aviation*, 2000. This and other reports on the economics of commercial aviation can be obtained at ATA's Web site at www.airlines.org.

2. Two strong analyses of what the government knew and when it knew it are Matthew Brzezinki's "Bust and Boom," *Washington Post*, 30 December 2001, p. W9 and Patrick Martin's "Was the U.S. Government Alerted to September 11 attack," [online], www.wsws.org/articles/2002/jan2002/sept.-j16_prn.shtml [January 2002].

3. David Sanger, "Two Leaders Tell of Plot to Kill Bush in Genoa," *New York Times*, 26 September 2001.

4. The FAA advisories in the summer of 2001 to the airlines regarding possible hijacking threats and the arrest of Zacarias Moussaoui were still not available to the public at the time of this writing.

5. White House Press Conference, 15 May 2002.

6. White House Press Conference, 16 May 2002.

7. Michael Isikoff and David Klaidman, "The Hijackers We Let Escape," *Newsweek*, 10 June 2002.

8. Ibid.

9. Norta Trulock, "Poorly Served," *Accuracy in Media,* [online] www. aim.org/publications/weekly_column/2002/05/23.html [23 May 2002].

10. Ibid.

11. Mark Fireman and Judy Pasternak, "Suicide Flights and Crop Dusters Considered Threats at '96 Olympics," *Los Angeles Times,* 17 November 2001.

12. Doug Struck et al., "Borderless Network of Terror, Bin Laden Followers Reach Across the Globe," *Washington Post,* 23 September 2001.

13. John K. Cooley, *Unholy Wars* (Sterling, Va.: Pluto Press, 1997), p. 247.

14. Dave Hirschman, *Hijacked: The True Story of the Heroes of Flight 705* (New York: William Morrow, 1997) provides a tremendous analysis of what happened during this failed suicide hijacking.

15. Steve Fainaru and James Grimaldi, "FBI Knew Terrorists Were Using Flight Schools," *Washington Post,* 23 September 2001.

16. To read more about Dr. Todd Curtis and his strong analysis of the events of 9/11, visit his Web site at www.AirSafe.com.

17. *Frankfurter Allgemeine Zeitung,* September 14, 2001.

18. Dennis Cauchon, "For Many on September 11, Survival Was No Accident," *USA Today,* 20 December 2001.

19. Ibid.

20. Nicholas Rufford, David Leppard, and Paul Eddy, "Nuclear Mystery: Crashed Plane's Target May Have Been Reactor," *London Times,* 21 October 2001.

21. Ibid.

22. Ibid.

23. AFL-CIO Layoff Tracker, "Economic Crisis Grows," [online], www.aflcio.org [January 2002].

24. "FBI: 9/11 Hijackers Cased Airports and Took Test Runs," *USA Today,* 29 May 2002.

25. Ibid.

26. Jennifer Rosinski and Jow Dwinell, "Woman Reflects on Seeing Atta," *Daily News Tribune,* [online], www.dailynewstribune.com/news/local_regional/sudb_atta05292002.htm [29 May 2002].

27. Ibid.

28. Paul Sperry, "Terrorists Slit Throats of 2 AA Stewardesses," WorldNetDaily.com, [online], www.worldnetdaily.com/article.asp?/article_id=24445 [16 June 2002].

28. This information comes from the FAA's Executive Summary of September 11, 2001. A complete copy of this document is included in appendix A at the back of this book.

29. A complete copy of FAA Order 8400.10 is included in appendix B at the back of this book.

30. To read about this and dozens of other similar references, my book *Air Rage: Crisis in the Skies* (Amherst, N.Y.: Prometheus Books, 2001) is one of the most comprehensive sources on the subject of disruptive passengers—at the risk of sounding arrogant.

31. Ibid.

32. Ibid.

33. Matthew Wald, " 'We Have Some Planes,' Hijacker Told Controller," *New York Times*, 16 October 2001.

34. Ibid.

35. Dan Eggen, "Airports Screened Nine of September 11 Hijackers," *Washington Post*, 2 March 2002, p. A11.

36. Chris Hansen, "Former FAA Special Agent Foresaw Problems at Logan Airport," NBC News, 16 September 2001.

37. Ibid.

# CHAPTER 2: THE CULTURE OF COMPROMISE

1. The complete reference for the *Federal Aviation Act of 1958* is Public Law 85-726; 72 Stat. 737; 49 U.S.C. App. 1301 *et. seq.*

2. Commission of Engineering and Technical Systems, 1999, "Assessment of Technologies Deployed to Improve Aviation Security, National Academy of Sciences," p. 17.

3. Ibid.

4. "The Revolving Door," *Miami Herald*, 11 November 2001.

5. Stephanie Mencimer, "Tom Daschle's Hillary Problem," *Washington Monthly* (January/February 2002).

6. Robert Kolker, "Passing the Buck: Who Shortchanged Airport Security?" NewYorkMetro.com, [online], www.newyorkmetro.com/news/article/wtc/kolker.htm [3 July 2002].

7. Walter Robinson and Glen Johnson, "Airlines Fought Security Changes Despite Warnings," *Boston Globe*, 20 September 2001.

8. Ibid.

9. Ibid.

10. On July 17, 1996, about 10:30 P.M. eastern daylight time, TWA flight 800, a Boeing 747-131, N93119, bound for Paris's Charles de Gaulle Airport, crashed in the Atlantic Ocean near East Moriches, New York. The flight departed New York's JFK International Airport about 10:10 P.M., with two pilots, two flight engineers, fourteen flight attendants, and 212 passengers on board. All 230 people on board were killed and the airplane was destroyed. The National Transportation Safety Board determined that the probable cause of the TWA flight 800 accident was an explosion of the center wing fuel tank (CWT), resulting from ignition of the flammable fuel/air mixture in the tank. The source of ignition energy for the explosion could not be determined with certainty, but, of the sources evaluated by the investigation, the most likely was a short circuit outside of the CWT. That short circuit allowed excessive voltage to enter the CWT through electrical wiring associated with the fuel quantity indication system. Contributing factors to the accident were the design-and-certification concept that fuel tank explosions could be prevented solely by precluding all ignition sources. The design and certification of the Boeing 747 has heat sources located beneath the CWT with no means to reduce the heat transferred into the CWT or to render the fuel vapor in the tank nonflammable.

11. A copy of the final report of the Gore Commission is available from a number of sources. One is www.airportnet.org/depts/regulatory/gorefinal.htm.

12. Walter Robinson and Glen Johnson, "Airlines Fought Security Changes Despite Warnings," *Boston Globe*, 20 September 2001.

13. Ibid.

14. For a complete version of the report "Delay, Dilute, and Discard: How the Airline Industry and the FAA Have Stymied Aviation Security Recommendations," visit Public Citizen's Web site at www.citizen.org/congess/regulations/issue_areas/faa/articles.cfm?ID=6215.

15. Written comments from TWA before the U.S. Department of Transportation, Federal Aviation Administration, Matter of Notice of Proposed Rulemaking on Employment History Verification and Criminal Records Check contained in the Docket No. FAA 1997-28859, 19 May 1997.

16. Letter from M. Victoria Cummock, Commissioner, White House

Commission on Aviation Safety and Security to Vice President Al Gore, Chairman, White House Commission on Aviation Safety and Security. See www.airportnet.org/depts/regulatory/gorefinal.htm.

17. A complete transcript of the December 7, 2000, meeting of the Aviation Security Advisory Committee can be obtained online at www.cas.faa.gov/readingroom/asacmeeting/min120700.pdf.

18. Peter Howe and Matthew Brelis, "Crashes in New York Had Grim Origins at Logan," *Boston Globe*, 12 September 2001.

19. Matthew Brelis and Matt Carroll, "FAA Finds Logan Security Among Worst in U.S.," *Boston Globe*, 26 September 2001.

20. Ibid.

21. Joe Battenfeld, "Massport Sex Scandal Results in Resignation," *Boston Herald*, 22 June 2000.

22. Ibid.

23. A copy of this letter appears in appendix C at the back of this book

24. Matthew Brelis and Sean Murphy, "FAA's Security Chief Out at Logan," *Boston Globe*, 29 September 2001.

25. Sean Murphy, "Logan Security Head Issued Warning," *Boston Globe*, 7 March 2002.

26. Ibid.

27. Interview with Deborah Sherman, 2 August 2002.

28. A copy of this letter appears in appendix D at the back of this book

29. Sean Murphy, "In Letter Before the Attacks, FAA Urged Easing Background Checks," *Boston Globe*, 12 December 2001.

30. A copy of this letter appears in appendix E at the back of this book.

31. Sean Murphy, "Logan Security Head Issued Warning," *Boston Globe*, 7 March 2002.

32. Sean Murphy, "FAA Put Security Testing on Hold," *Boston Globe*, 9 December 2001.

33. A copy of this e-mail appears in appendix F at the back of this book.

34. A copy of this e-mail appears in appendix G at the back of this book.

# CHAPTER 3: THE GREAT BAILOUT

1. "Bailout Showed the Weight of a Mighty and Fast-Acting Lobby," *Seniors USA*, [online], www.senrs.com/airline_bailout_result_of_powerful_lobby.htm [10 October 2001].

2. Ibid.

3. Associated Press, "Experts: The Airline Bailout Was Wrong," www.cgi.wn.com/article=12542643 [18 March 2002].

4. Jayne O'Donnell, "Is Support for American-BA Linkup Paid For?" *USA Today*, 18 January 2002.

5. Ibid.

6. Ibid.

7. Kate Randall, "How the U.S. Airlines Got the $15 Billion Bailout," World Socialist Web Site, [online], www.wsws.org/articles/2001/air-018_prn.shtml [10 October 2001].

8. Testimony of the Air Transport Association on the Financial Condition of the Airline Industry, U.S. House of Representatives Committee on Transportation and Infrastructure, 19 September 2001.

9. Ibid.

10. Ibid.

11. Ibid.

12. *Air Transportation Safety and System Stabilization Act*, Public Law 107-42, 49 USC 40101.

13. U.S. Senator Peter G. Fitzgerald, "Who Will Bail Out the American Taxpayer?" [online], http://fitzgerald.senate.gov/legislation/airbailout/oped [16 November 2001].

14. "Bailout Showed the Weight of a Mighty and Fast-Acting Lobby."

15. Hoovers Online, "Airlines Don't See Relief Over the Horizon," [online], www.hoovers.com/fp.asp?la..._id=NR200209071180.3_2b4e00 42b6ecfe72 [September 7, 2002].

16. Ibid.

17. BBC Business News, "Aviation Jobs Losses Reach 400,000," www.news.bbc.co.uk/hi/english/business/newsid_17773000/1773253.stm [11 January 2002].

18. J. D. Tuccille, "The Baneful Bailout," [online], www.free-market.net/spotlight/bailout/.

19. Michael Higgins, "Airlines' Cuts Anger Congress," *Chicago Tribune*, 27 October 2001.

20. Ibid.

21. Dan Reed, "Airlines to Get Millions in Refunds After Bailout," *Knight-Ridder News Service*, 7 March 2002.

22. Ibid.

23. U.S. Department of Transportation, Press Release Number 98-01a (Revised), 16 September 2001.

24. Mike Dorning, "Airlines Dominate Teams Studying Safeguards," *Chicago Tribune*, 24 September 2001.

25. Gary Stoller, "Official Says Air Task Force May Violate Law," *USA Today*, 20 September 2001.

26. Dorning, "Airlines Dominate Teams Studying Safeguards."

# CHAPTER 4: THE AVIATION SECURITY RESPONSE TO 9/11

1. Pete Hamill, "Air Safety Spins Out of Control," *New York Daily News*, 15 October 2001.

2. A copy of this e-mail appears in appendix H at the back of this book.

3. Jim Morris, "FAA Maintains Its Security Chief Leaving Voluntarily," *Dallas Morning News*, 9 October 2001.

4. Ibid.

5. Blake Morrison and Alan Levin, "FAA Security Chief Quits Over Assignment," *USA Today*, 11 October 2001.

6. Mike Fish, "Airport Security: A System Driven by the Minimum Wage," CNN [online], www.cnn.com/specials/trade.center/flight.risk/stories/part1 [20 October 2001].

7. Ibid.

8. Ibid.

9. Remarks of Carol B. Hallett, president and CEO of Air Transport Association of America, Inc. to the TIA Marketing Outlook Forum 2001 Atlanta, Ga., 2 October 2001.

10. The letter was signed by Patricia Friend, president of the Association of Flight Attendants; John Ward, president of the Association of Pro-

fessional Flight Attendants; Captain Robert Miller, president of the Independent Pilots Association; Joan Claybrook, president of the Public Citizen; Kevin Mitchell, president of the Business Travel Coalition; Nancy McKinley, manager of consumer and industry affairs, International Airline Passenger Association; Bob Monetti, member of the FAA Aviation Security Advisory Committee; and Paul Hudson, executive director of the Aviation Consumer Action Project (ACAP). A full text can be obtained at www.citizen. org/print_article.cfm?ID=6398.

11. Susan E. Dudley, "Regulation, Post-9/11," *National Review*, 26 March 2002.

12. "Public Optimism Growing in War on Terror," [online], www. publicagenda.org/specials/terrorism/121701terror_pubopinion.htm [17 December 2001].

13. Mike Fish, "Airport Security Debate Focuses on Government's Role," CNN [online], www.cnn.com/specials/trade.center/flight.risk/ stories/part4 [17 November 2001].

14. Remarks by President George W. Bush at the signing of Aviation Security Legislation, Ronald Reagan National Airport, Washington, D.C., 19 November 2001.

15. The assumption of civil aviation security functions and responsibilities of the Transportation Security Administration is found under Chapter 449, Title 49, U.S.C.

## CHAPTER 5: THE BUSINESS OF AVIATION AND THE NEW SECURITY REGIMEN

1. Findings of the Air Transport Action Group (ATAG), *The Economic Benefits of Air Transport*, January 2000, Geneva, Switzerland.

2. Laurence Zuckerman, "A New Sense of Urgency in Debating the Future of Airlines," *New York Times*, 17 December 2001.

3. Carol Hallett, "Winging It Through Stormy Times," *Washington Times*, 10 July 2002.

4. Zuckerman, "A New Sense of Urgency in Debating the Future of Airlines."

5. Walter Woods, "Security Costs Prolonging Delta's Malaise," *Atlanta Business Chronicle*, 6 September 2002.

6. Ibid.

7. Ibid.

8. "Airline Relief Bill Clears House Panel," *Washington Post,* 3 October 2002, p. E2.

9. Carol B. Hallett, "Requests for Aid Justified," op-ed for *USA Today,* 27 September 2002.

10. Ibid.

11. "Airline Relief Bill Clears House Panel."

12. "Airlines return to Congress," CNN [online], http://cnn.all politics.p...5386&partnerID=2001 [24 September 2002].

13. Keith Alexander, "U.S. Security Fees Weigh on Airlines," *Washington Post,* 6 September 2002, p. E1.

14. Edward Wong, "Airlines Are Now Asking U.S. to Cut Back on Security Measures," *New York Times,* 13 September 2002.

15. "Airlines' Pleas for Help Land Poorly Amid Political Gifts," *USA Today,* 2 October 2002.

16. "9/11 Doesn't Excuse Airlines' Bad Business Decisions," *USA Today,* 27 September 2002.

## CHAPTER 6: CONCERNS ABOUT THE NEW AVIATION SECURITY SYSTEM

1. Greg Schneider and Sara Kehaulani Goo, "Twin Missions Overwhelmed TSA," *Washington Post,* 3 September 2002, p. A1.

2. House Committee on Government Reform, "Progress in Implementing Provisions of the Aviation and Transportation Security Act," report prepared by Alexis M. Stefani, 7 August 2002.

3. Kevin Johnson, "Aviation Security Drains Agencies," *USA Today,* 11 July 2002.

4. Schnieder and Goo, "Twin Missions."

5. Initial contact between the author and Mr. Warren took place during a telephone conversation on April 3, 2002. On April 16, 2002, Mr. Warren left his voicemail message at the author's number.

6. Blake Morrison, "Airport Security Failures Persist: Simulated Weapons Slip by 1 in 4 times," *USA Today,* 2 May 2002, p. A1.

7. Paul Sperry, "FAA Whistleblower Slams New Airport Security

Law," WorldNetDaily.com, [online], www.worldnetdaily.com/news/
article.asp?ARTICLE_ID=25455 [27 November 2001].

8. Ibid.

9. "The $16 Billion Soft Landing," *Common Cause*, [online], www.
commoncause.org/publications/jan02/ 010302.hrm [10 January 2002].

10. Schneider and Goo, "Twin Missions."

11. Ibid.

12. Ibid.

13. "The $16 Billion Soft Landing."

14. Ibid.

15. Seth Borenstein, "Airline Security Criticism Grows," *Salt Lake Tribune* [online], www.sltrib.com/2002/jul/07202002/nation_w/755170.
htm [20 July 2002].

16. House Subcommittee on Transportation and Architecture, statement of Norman Mineta, Secretary of Transportation, 23 July 2002.

17. Jonathan Salant, "Mineta Holds Options on Lockheed," *Washington Post*, 22 July 2002.

18. *The Center for Responsive Politics* [online], www.opensecrets.org.

19. Ibid.

20. Charles Slepian, interviewed by the author, September 2002.

21. "One Year Later, Scattershot Fixes Hamper Air Security," *USA Today*, September 9, 2002.

22. James Aldridge, "Trade Group Blasts Feds' Cargo Security Measures," *San Antonio Business Journal*, 5 July 2002.

23. Janelle House, "Anti-terrorism Expert Says U.S. Should Pro-react, Not Just React," *Baxter Bulletin*, 7 October 2002.

24. Mike Wendling, "Aviation Still Vulnerable One Year After 9/11," [online], www.cnsnews.com/nation/archive/200209/nat20020911a.
html [9 September 2002].

25. Ibid.

26. Sara Kehaulani Goo, "Fledging TSA Offers Lessons," *Washington Post*, 22 July 2002.

27. House Subcommittee on Transportation and Architecture, statement of Norman Mineta, Secretary of Transportation, 23 July 2002.

28. Associated Press, "Loy Adjusting Airport Restrictions," *Washington Post*, 10 October 2002.

29. Ibid.

## CHAPTER 7: RISK ANALYSIS AND AVIATION SECURITY

1. Some of the ideas for this scenario come from the manufacturers of the CRUPAX cockpit door system. For more information, visit them at www.p-cel.com.

2. Bruce Scheiner, *Counterpane* e-newsletter, 15 April 2002. To subscribe, go to www.counterpane.com/crypto-gram-0204.html.

## CHAPTER 8: AVIATION AND VIOLENCE

1. "Plane Crash Near Here Tuesday Night Kills 7," *Chesteron Tribune*, 12 October 1933.

2. Ibid.

3. Peter Grier, "Flight-crew Sabotage Can Be Hard to Prove," *Christian Science Monitor*, 18 November 1999.

4. Ehud Sprinzak, "Rational Fanatics," *Foreign Policy* (September–October 2001).

5. Dr. Bruce Hoffman, "Aviation Security and Terrorism: An Analysis of the Potential Threat to Air Cargo Interrogators," Centre for the Study of Terrorism and Political Violence, St. Andrews University, Scotland, September 1997.

6. Ibid.

7. This is the same definition that was used in my previous book, *Air Rage: Crisis in the Skies* (Amherst, N.Y.: Prometheus Books, 2001).

8. Comments from Gerald Brave, Organized Crime and Rackets Bureau, Assistant District Attorney, Queens, New York, [online], www.queensda.org/Divisions%20and%20Bureaus/Investigations%20Division/Organized%20Crimes%20and%20Rackets.htm [July 2001].

9. "Richard Reid Pleads Guilty Faces Minimum Sentence of 60 Years," CNN [online], www.cnn.com/2002/LAW/10/04/reid.guilty.plea/index.html [5 October 2002].

10. "Jack Gilbert Graham," FBI Famous Cases [online], www.fbi.gov/libref/historic/famcases.

11. "15-Year-Old Commandeers Aircraft," CNN [online], www.cnn.com/2002/US/01/06/tampa.crash [6 January 2002].

12. "Disruptive Passenger Released to Halfway House," *Naples Daily*

*News*, 21 August 2002.

13. Pedro Ruiz Guitierrez, "Terror Fears Force Plane to Return to Orlando," *Orlando Sentinel*, 27 September 2002.

14. Maline Hazle, "Pilot Ousts Sheriff from SF Flight," *Record Searchlight* [online], www.redding.com/news/past/20020925toplo007.shtml [25 September 2002].

15. Reuters, "Man Tries to Strangle Flight Attendant," 29 August 2002.

16. "Drunk Sparks Hijack Alert," CNN [online], www.cnn.com/2002/WORLD/europe/07/19/spain.hijack/ [19 July 2002].

17. These were available at Hartsfield's Web site: www.atlanta-airport.com.

18. "Airport Shooter's Wife Blames U.S.," www.cbsnews.com/stories/2002/07/04/national/main 514292.shtml [4 July 2002]/

19. Alva Viarruel, "Cocaine Found on BWIA Plane in Canada," *Trinidad Express* [online], 209.94.197.2/sept/sept9/general.htm [9 September 1998].

# CHAPTER 9: VULNERABILITIES OF THE AVIATION SECURITY SYSTEM

1. Daniel Dombey, "EU Bickering Delays Airport Security Plans," *Financial Times*, 3 July 2002.

2. Tony Thompson, "People Traffickers Bribe Airport Guards to Beat Passport Checks," *The Observor*, 22 September 2002.

3. Kathleen Koch, "FAA: 157 Airspace Violations Since 9/11," CNN, 21 September 2002.

4. Ibid.

5. "Plug Holes in Air Security," *USA Today*, 8 July 2002.

6. Richard A. Mueller, "Crop Duster Terrorism," *MIT Technology Review*, 11 March 2002.

7. Daniel G. Fricker, "Terrorists Stealing Airline Uniforms and Credentials, Pilot Group Says," *Detroit Free Press*, 3 July 2002.

8. Ibid.

9. Leslie Miller, "Air Attendants Want Better Training," *Newsday*, 5 September 2002.

10. Ibid.

# CHAPTER 10: AVIATION SECURITY MEASURES

1. "Airport Security Report," *Airport Weekly*, 9 October 2002.
2. Ibid.
3. Bruce Schneier is the best-selling author of the benchmark work *Secrets and Lies: Digital Security in a Networked World* (New York: John Wiley & Sons, 2000). His five-step process for security-measure evaluation was described in the *Counterpane* e-newsletter on 15 April 2002. To subscribe: www.counterpane.com/crypto-gram-0204.html.
4. Sherrie Gossett, "Baggage Screening: Millions Spent on Illusion of Safety?" [online], www.worldnetdaily.com/article.asp?ARTICLEID=28373 [23 July 2002].
5. Dr. Bogdan Castle Maglich, "Best Kept Secret of FAA: FAA's Certified X-Ray 'Explosive Detector Systems' Cannot Detect Explosives," draft, 31 December 2001.
6. Sherrie Gossett, "Baggage Screening: Millions Spent on Illusion of Safety?"
7. Ibid.
8. Hiawatha Bray, "Face Testing at Logan Is Found Lacking," *Boston Globe*, 17 July 2002.
9. Ibid.
10. Bruce Schneier, *Counterpane*, e-newsletter, 15 May 2002.
11. Lauren Weinstein, "Register Air Travelers?" *Wired Digital*, 7 October 2002.

# CHAPTER 11: MAKING SENSE OF IT ALL

1. Parts of this "press conference" were originally published at The Onion.com, www.theonion.com/onion3838/faa_passenger_ban.html.
2. Thomas C. Schelling, foreword to *Pearl Harbor: Warning and Decision*, by Roberta Wohlstetter (Palo Alto, Calif.: Stanford University Press, 1962).
3. Oliver Burkeman, "Can We Ever Stop This?" *Guardian*, 28 September 2001.

# INDEX

# AVIATION INSECURITY NEWSLETTER

## written and published by Andrew R. Thomas

**A** free monthly e-newsletter that provides news, summaries, analyses, insights, and commentarites on aviation safety and security.

Written in a similar style to this book, the e-newsletter provides timely updates to aviation security issues, interesting links, breaking news, and general commentary. Join the more than forty thousand readers who get aviation safety and security information from the *Aviation Insecurity E-Newsletter*.

To subscribe, please visit www.AviationInsecurity.com

*Andrew R. Thomas and AviationInsecurity.com will NOT use the e-newsletter mailing list for any other purpose than e-mailing the newsletter. We will NOT use the mailing list for product marketing, nor will we sell the list to any third parties.*

## ALSO BY ANDREW R. THOMAS

*Air Rage: Crisis in the Skies*

*Defining the Really Great Boss*
(with M. David Dealy)

*Global Manifest Destiny*
(with John A. Caslione)

*Growing Your Business in Emerging Markets*
(with John A. Caslione)

*The Rise of Women Entrepreneurs: People, Processes, and Global Trends*
(with Jeanne Halladay-Coughlin)